Tikkun Shechinah

Written By Reb Moshe Steinerman

Edited by Elise Teitelbaum

Tikkun Shechinah

Ilovetorah Jewish Outreach Network

iloveTorah Jewish Publishing
First Published 2018
ISBN: 978-1-947706-08-8

Copyright: ilovetorah Jewish Publishing
www.ilovetorah.com
moshe@ilovetorah.com

All Rights reserved

Editor: Elise Teitelbaum
Co Editor: Rochel Steinerman

No part of this publication may be translated, reproduced, stored in a retrieval system or transmitted, in any form or by any means, electronic, mechanical, photocopying, recording or otherwise, without prior permission in writing from Reb Moshe Steinerman.
Artwork by Boris Shapiro
Book Format By Rabbi Benyamin Fleischman

ABOUT THE AUTHOR

Rabbi Moshe Steinerman grew up as a religious Jew on the hillsides of Maryland. During his teenage years, Reb Moshe developed his talent for photography, while connecting to nature and speaking to *HaShem*. He later found his path through Breslov *Chassidus*, while maintaining closeness to the *Litvish* style of learning. He studied in the Baltimore yeshiva, Ner Yisrael; then married and moved to Lakewood, New Jersey. After settling down, he began to write *Kavanos Halev*, with the blessing of *Rav* Malkiel Kotler *Shlita*, Rosh Yeshiva of Beis Medrash Gevoha.

After establishing one of the first Jewish outreach websites, iloveTorah.com in 1996, Reb Moshe's teachings became popular among the full spectrum of Jews, from the unaffiliated to ultra-Orthodox. His teachings, including hundreds of stories of tzaddikim, gained popularity due to the ideal of drawing Jews together. Reb Moshe made aliyah to Tzfat in 2003 and returned many English-speaking Jews to Judaism through his hundreds of Jewish videos and audio shiurim. His learning experience includes the completion of both Talmud Bavli and Yerushalmi as well as other important works.

In 2012, Reb Moshe, with his wife and children, moved to Jerusalem. Some of his other books are Kavalos Halev (Meditations of the Heart), Prayers of the Heart, Tovim Meoros (Glimpse of Light), Chassidus, Kabbalah & Meditation, Yom Leyom (Day by Day), Pathways of the Righteous, A Journey into Holiness, and The True Intentions of the Baal Shem Tov. Thousands have read the advice contained in these books, with life-changing results.

Special thanks to Rabbi Benyamin Fleischman for making the books into print-ready format and to Elise Teitelbaum for helping to edit the books.

*In Memory of my father Shlomo Zavel Ben Yaakov zt"l
And all the great souls of our people*

I grew up in a house filled with the *Torah* learning of my father, who studied most of the day. Although there were no Jews in this remote part of Maryland, my father was a man of *chesed* to all people and was known for his brilliance in *Torah* scholarship.

I want to say a special thank you to the Nikolsberg Rebbe and the Biala Rebbe for their encouragement and blessings. Most of all, I offer thanks to my wife, Rochel, for her faithful support.

*Dedicated to my wife Rochel
and to my children Shlomo Nachman, Yaakov Yosef, Gedalya Aharon Tzvi, Esther Rivka, Yeshiya Michel, Dovid Shmuel, Eliyahu Yisrael
may it bring forth the light of your neshamos.*

In Memory of Tom and Eva Rona from the Crawford Family.

In Memory of Masha bas Avraham

In Memory of Menachem Ben Ruvein, Toba Esther Bas Gedalya Aharon HaKohein, Yaakov Ben Shlomo Zavel, Yehuda Ben Ike

Reb Moshe Steinerman

DEAR READER,

Ilovetorah Jewish Outreach is a non-profit and books and Torah classes are available at low costs. Therefore, we appreciate your donation to help Rabbi Moshe Steinerman and ilovetorah to continue their work on behalf of the Jewish people. We also ask that you pass on these books to others once you are finished with them.

Thank you,
Reb Moshe Steinerman
www.ilovetorah.com
Donations
www.ilovetorah.com/donations

RABBINIC APPROVALS / HASKAMAHS
The Baila Rebbe

הובא לפני גליונות בעניני קירוב רחוקים לקרב אחינו בני ישראל אל אביהם שבשמים, כידוע מהבעש"ט זיע"א שאמר "אימתי קאתי מר לכשיפוצו מעינותיך חוצה" ואפריון נמטי"ה להאי גברא יקירא מיקירי צפת עיה"ק תובב"א כמעל"כ מוהר"ר משה שטיינרמן שליט"א אשר כבר עוסק רבות בשנים לקרב רחוקים לתורה וליהדות, ועת מוציא לאור ספר בשם "תיקון השכינה" וראיתי דברים נחמדים מאוד וניכר מתוך הדברים שהרב בעל המחבר - אהבת השי"ת ואהבת התורה וישראל בלבבו, ובטחוני כי הספר יביא תועלת גדולה לכל עם ישראל.

ויה"ר שיזכה לבוא לגומרה ברוב פאר והדר ונזכה לגאולתן של ישראל בב"א.

בכבוד רב:
אהרן שלמה חיים אליעזר
בלאאמו"ר הגה"ה אבי"שלא

Reb Moshe Steinerman

Rabbi M. Lebovits
Grand Rabbi of
Nikolsburg
53 Decatur Avenue
Spring Valley, N.Y. 10977

יוסף יחיאל מיכל
לעבאוויטש
ניקלשבורג
מאנסי - ספרינג וואלי, נ.י.

בעזהשי"ת

בשורותי אלו באתי להעיד על מעשה אמן, מופלא מופלג בהפלגת חכמים ונבונים, ירא וחרד לדבר ה', ומשתוקק לקרב לבית ישראל לאביהם שבשמים, ה"ה הרב **משה שטיינערמאן** שליט"א בעיה"ק צפת תובב"א

שעלה בידו להעלות על הספר דברים נפלאים שאסף מספרים הקדושים, בענין אהבה אחוה שלום ורעות, לראות מעלות חברינו ולא חסרונם, ועי"ז נמנעים מדברי ריבות ומחלוקת, ולתקן עון שנאת חנם אשר בשביל זה נחרב בית מקדשינו ותפארתינו, וכמשאחז"ל (ויקרא רבה פ' ט) על ויחן שם ישראל, שניתנה תורה באופן שחנו שם כאיש אחד בלב אחד.

וניכר בספר כי עמל ויגע הרבה להוציא מתח"י דבר נאה ומתוקן, ע"כ אף ידי תכון עמו להוציאו לאור עולם, יהי רצון שחפץ ה' בידו יצליח, יברך ה' חילו ופועל ידי תרצה, שיתברך על המוגמר להגדיל תורה ולהאדירה ולהפיצו בקרב ישראל, עד ביאת גוא"צ בב"א.

א"ד הכותב לכבוד התורה ומרביציה,
י"ט חשון תשס"ו

Tikkun Shechinah

Rabbi Abraham Y. S. Friedman
161 Maple Avenue #C Spring Valley NY 10977
Tel: 845-425-5043 Fax: 845-425-8045

בעזהשי"ת

ישפות השם החיים והשלו', לכבוד ידידי מאז ומקדם מיקירי קרתא דירושלים יראה שלם, זוכה ומזכה אחרים, להיות דבוק באלקינו, ה"ה הר"ר משה שטיינרמאן שליט"א.

שמחתי מאוד לשמוע ממך, מאתר רחוק וקירוב הלבבות, בעסק תורתך הקדושה ועבודתך בלי לאות, וכה יעזור ה' להלאה ביתר שאת ויתר עז. והנה שלחת את הספר שלקטת בעניני דביקות בה', לקרב לבבות בני ישראל לאבינו שבשמים בשפת אנגלית, אבל דא עקא השפת לא ידעינו, ע"כ לא זכיתי לקרותו, ע"כ א"א לי ליתן הסכמה פרטי על ספרך, ובכלל קיבלתי על עצמי שלא ליתן הסכמות, ובפרט כשאין לי פנאי לקרות הספר מתחלתו עד סופו, אבל בכלליות זכרתי לך חסד נעוריך, היאך הי' המתיקות שלך בעבדות השם פה בעירינו, ובנועם המדות, וחזקה על חבר שאינו מוציא מתחת ידו דבר שאינו מתוקן, ובפרט שכל מגמתך להרבות כבוד שמים, שבוודאי סייעתא דשמיא ילוך כל ימיך לראות רב נחת מיוצ"ח ומפרי ידיך, שתתקבל הספר בסבר פנים יפות אצל אחינו בני ישראל שמדברים בשפת האנגלית שיתקרבו לאבינו שבשמים ולהדבק בו באמת כאות נפשך, ולהרבות פעלים לתורה ועבודה וקדושה בדביקות עם מדות טובות, בנייחותא נייחא בעליונים ונייחא בתחתונים עד ביאת גואל צדק בב"א.

כ"ד ידידך השמח בהצלחתך ובעבודתך

Reb Moshe Steinerman

בס"ד

RABBI DOVID B. KAPLAN
RABBI OF WEST NEW YORK
5308 Palisade Avenue • West New York, NJ 07093
201-807-6859 • WestNewYorkShul@Gmail.com

דוד ברוך הלוי קאפלאן
רב ואב"ד דק"ק
וועסט ניו יארק

י' שבט ה'תשע"ז / February 6, 2017

Dear Friends,

Shalom and Blessings!

For approximately twenty years I have followed the works of Rabbi Moshe Steinerman, Shlit"a, a pioneer in the use of social media to encourage people and bring them closer to G-d.

Over the years Rabbi Steinerman has produced, and made public at no charge, hundreds of videos sharing his Torah wisdom, his holy stories, and his touching songs. Rabbi Steinerman has written a number of books, all promoting true Jewish Torah spirituality. Rabbi Steinerman's works have touched many thousands of Jews, and even spirituality-seeking non-Jews, from all walks of life and at all points of the globe.

Rabbi Steinerman is a tomim (pure-hearted one) in the most flattering sense of the word.

I give my full approbation and recommendation to all of Rabbi Steinerman's works.

I wish Rabbi Steinerman much success in all his endeavors.

May G-d bless Rabbi Moshe Steinerman, his wife, Rebbetzin Rochel Steinerman, and their beautiful children; and may G-d grant them health, success, and nachas!

With blessings,

Rabbi Dovid B. Kaplan

TABLE OF CONTENTS

ABOUT THE AUTHOR 3
DEAR READER, ... 5
RABBINIC APPROVALS / HASKAMAHS 6
TABLE OF CONTENTS 10
INTRODUCTION 14
INTRODUCTION FROM THE SHECHINAH 18
PART ONE 19

Comfort You 19
SUCCESS 22
KABBALAS SHABBOS 25
TORAH LISHMAH 27
COMING DOWN TO US 29
ALONE AT NIGHT 31
EVIL THOUGHTS 33
SLANDER/LOSHON HARA 35
IS THERE PEACE? 37
HUGE STONE 39
MY CHILD 42
RESPECTING/TRUSTING TZADDIKIM 44
HAPPINESS 46

YOU FORGOT ME	48
IMPROVING YOUR MEMORY	50
FINAL REDEMPTION	52
THE SHECHINAHS HOME	54
HOLINESS IN SPEECH	57
EATING WITH THE SHECHINAH	59
ONE'S LIVELIHOOD	61
YOMIM TOVIM, A great time!	64
SPIRITUALITY OF MUSIC	66
DON'T TRAVEL WITHOUT ME	68
TZITZIS	70
SWEETENING JUDGMENT	72
PERFECT SIMPLICITY	74
LAZINESS	76
HOLINESS OF TEFILLIN	78
CHESED	80
BRINGING A FINAL PEACE	82
SHIDDUCHIM	84
BENIFITS OF HALACHA	87

ANGER	89
CHANNELS OF BLESSING	91
HOSPITALITY	93
WORRIES OF THE HEART	95
WOMEN & THE SHECHINAH	97
THE MATERIAL WORLD	100
CONNECTION TO SHABBOS	102
CHANNELING ILLNESS	104
EMPTINESS	106
CAN I REALLY KNOW YOU?	108
DO YOU SURROUND ME	110
YOUR PRESENCE UPON ME	112
MY THOUGHTS	113
MODESTY	114
PART TWO	116
SHECHINAH, THE SECRET ELEVATION	116
PART THREE	125
TIKKUN CHATZOS AND CONNECTING TO THE SHECHINAH	125
PART FOUR	135
STORIES ABOUT THOSE WHO AROSE DURING THE NIGHT	135
PART FIVE	144
INTRODUCTION TO TIKKUN ROCHEL AND LEAH	144
PART SIX	149

TIKKUN ROCHEL AND TIKKUN LEAH.......................... 149
TIKKUN RACHEL... 149
TIKKUN LEAH... 166
PRAYERS AT CHATZOS BY REB MOSHE.................... 183
2000 YEARS ARE ENOUGH, THE KOTEL CRIES OUT!
.... 183
.... 183
OY SALVATION.. 184
ARISE, CRY OUT!... 185
AT NIGHT HIS SONG IS WITH ME 186
HOW MUCH LONGER?.. 187
REBUILD OUR HOUSE!.. 188
GLOSSARY **189**

INTRODUCTION

Should your heart be open and your mind clear, this *sefer* has but one objective for you: to reunite you with *HaShem* and the *Shechinah* in ways that will enrich your life, both in your religious worship and your day-to-day activities.

As in the beginning of all reunions, there is much to learn about one another, and a deeper understanding is needed to reunite harmoniously. We must begin by humbling ourselves to receive what the *Shechinah* has to offer, as elucidated in this book. There is so much we have to learn about the *Shechinah* - in fact, we do not realize what truly amazing things await us!

The Hebrew word *Shechinah* can be translated to mean "Divine Presence". When *HaShem* created the world, He also created the concept of the *Shechinah*, a constricted light that emanated from Him so that man could attach himself to *HaShem*. When Adam sinned in *Gan Eden*, *HaShem* sent the *Shechinah* to accompany him into exile, to protect and help him return to the proper ways.

We can think of the relationship between *HaShem* and the *Shechinah* as similar to that of the sun to the moon. *HaShem* is like the sun. The sun is too bright and powerful for the human eye to look at unaided, especially the closer you get to it. With the use of certain filters scientists can look directly at the sun, as these filters cause the light of the sun to be dimmed. The same principle can be applied to the light of *HaShem*. The cleaner and purer one's heart, the more directly he can look into *HaShem's* light. *HaShem* also provides us with spiritual "sunglasses" to give us shade, allowing us to get closer to His light. By trying our best to perform the 613 commandments, we can gain a measure of shade for our spiritual "eyes".

The *Shechinah* is often compared to the moon. It is the feminine aspect of *HaShem* - the accessible version of *HaShem's* light, available to all. One can look directly at the moon and easily see its light. We can see the moon both day and night, but most easily at night, when the world is in darkness. *Shechinah,* the moon, may disappear behind the clouds in our lives, but we know that She is there, waiting for us. She is also regarded as mother to *Bnai Yisrael.* When we hurt, so does She. The *Shechinah* bears alone much of the pain of the *galus* for us, as the full burden would be too much. She is like a mother grieving over the pains of Her children. She yearns to comfort us but, unaware of her presence and Her real importance, we very much ignore Her - not understanding how to connect. This *sefer* serves to help us build a relationship between man and the *Shechinah*; to reunite us with our mother.

One thing we must realize is that the *Shechinah* is for us. She was sent into exile by *HaShem* to be with Her children, to benefit us with Her greatness and light. We were born to receive that light from Her; it is very much the purpose of our existence. *HaShem's* will in creating us was to shine His light, to share with us the greatness of His existence. One can only imagine how much more light is reserved for the righteous in *Gan Eden.* The *Shechinah* is our connection to *HaShem* - it is the constricted light of *HaShem.*

Since the *Shechinah* is there for us, certainly we can feel Her light and connect with Her at every moment. We must also take upon ourselves the responsibility of elevating Her. For too long, she has been cast aside like a stranger. Ignorant of Her presence, we neither cared for Her, nor appreciated Her. We have not known our own mother and walk around all our lives like orphans, not knowing She exists. By performing the *mitzvos,* studying Torah, and purifying ourselves, we are able to rekindle this important relationship.

Within this *sefer,* we have gathered from our sages some of the greatest and most inspirational teachings about the *Shechinah.* We have also shed light on much of the mystery about Her, opening our eyes to a strength otherwise unknown to us. Through the learning of *Tikkun Shechinah*, you can aid in the *tikkun olam* and attain a greater level of self-perfection with the guidance of the *Shechinah* herself. This is truly an original work and an important one.

Yours Truly,
Reb Moshe Steinerman of Safed, Yerushalayim

DRAWING BY MY SISTER TRUMAH KUGLER

Our sages teach us that the Temple will be rebuilt by the merit of those who remember and mourn over her pain. We can learn from the Shechinah far more then we truly realize.

INTRODUCTION FROM THE SHECHINAH

My dearest children, it brings Me great pleasure to know that your heart is open to knowing Me. For too long we have been like strangers. Your Father sent Me away from Him so that I should be together with you because of the many transgressions of the world, we too have become separated from one another. I feel so alone, as not only have I gone into exile away from your Father but now you, My children, are like orphans who never knew their Mother.

    I want you to know that I have always been here for you. Even in the darkest places, even there you can learn to know Me; how much more so in places full of light and holiness. We haven't been close as of yet, due to a deficiency in *yiras HaShem*. Let this no longer be an obstacle separating all of us. My only desire has been to take you in My arms and hold you, to show you holy lights unknown to you. I want to draw you close to your Father, and end this exile forever.

    There is so much a mother wants to express to her child. I have not been able to express and connect to you since you were little, free of sin. This opportunity now I value dearly, knowing your ears can be opened to My voice.

    May it be the Almighty's will that through the wisdom and advice in this *sefer* we can reunite with each other, I with My Husband, and you with your Father.

Yours Truly,
The Shechinah

PART ONE

Comfort You

Holy *Shechinah*, how may I comfort You?
    All I want to know is that you are making a conscious effort to change your ways for the better.

What faults should I work most closely to overcome?
    Pride. If you did not have so much pride, then you wouldn't sin. When a person does a wrongful deed, it is because he feels he deserves something more than what he has been given. A humble person realizes how lucky he is to have been given the blessings he has; one with pride ignores all good and will never be happy.

Sometimes I feel lost, why?
    It becomes difficult for you to feel My presence when you are mired in worldly affairs. I am still there, though, by your side. You feel lost because you sense I have left you completely, but this is really the action of the *Satan*, who feeds you feelings of depression and low self-worth. I would never abandon my children.

So, when we sin, You are there?
    I am there, holding on to the little that remains of your holy *neshamah*. No matter what you do, you can never

reverse the holiness that comes with being a Jew. Even if you dig yourself into the lowest pit, I am there to protect you if you seek Me. There is always a spark of good in evil; it just needs to be separated and pursued. When you are tempted by sin, but you choose the path of good, much blessing will descend on you through the upper worlds. Should you choose to continue on the path of evil, not only do you hurt yourself; you also cause damage to all of these worlds. When you sin, you drag Me down with you because I cannot leave My children. You can't feel Me because you are too preoccupied with the pleasure of sin. Should you take a moment to stop and look around, you would see Me there. Certainly, you would not continue your actions then.

If we make the mistake of committing a negative commandment, what should we do to correct ourselves?

Repent and take measures to ensure that you don't do this horrible action again. Begin to feel remorse and confess right away your mistake to *HaShem*. Make a list of ways you can avoid making this mistake again. Then smile.

I don't understand. We just committed an act of treason, yet we are to be happy?

The entire purpose of the *Satan's* pushing you into sin was to draw you further into depression. He has already tripped you once; shall we let him continue to treat you like his slave? By taking corrective action and then smiling, we show that you have not given in to the feelings of despair and self-hatred.

Still, how can I be happy when I have just destroyed my *neshamah*, and brought harm upon all the worlds and myself?

The harm you have done to the upper worlds can be rectified immediately. Do not wait. Pick yourself up and be joyous in *HaShem*. Start dancing and surround yourself with positive commandments! When an opponent feels he has won, he immediately begins to rejoice. Should you quickly surmount yourself, you become completely free from him. So distracted is he with the thought of victory that you can now climb to the highest of worlds without further hindrance.

SUCCESS

Shechinah, how can I be a successful person?
First you must decide what success is. It cannot always be viewed clearly in the eyes of the beholder. Many people automatically assume themselves to be unsuccessful. Success can mean many things, and be weighed in various ways.

Well, how do I tell how successful I am? I honestly feel I have not accomplished that which I should.
How are you to know exactly what _HaShem_ wants from you? Maybe all He wanted is to know that you are trying the best you can. Real success is not how much one actually has accomplished, but how much he changes through trying. _HaShem_ has seen all your hard work, your trials and your effort. You are successful, in that you have done your best.

I do not feel I have done the best I could. I've wasted so much time and emotional strength, only to come up short in my own goals and expectations.
Yes but, nonetheless, you had the sincere desire to do as you were commanded by _HaShem_. This counts for a lot in _HaShem's_ view, as "The sacrifices _HaShem_ desires are a broken spirit; a heart broken and humbled, Oh _HaShem_, You will not despise."[1]

---

[1] Psalms 51:19

How can I advance to the next level, where not only am I trying the best I can, but I am also accomplishing what I set out to do?

Simply stay close to Me. If I am with you, then everything you do will be accompanied by the blessing of success. Things that were only a dream to you will slowly come forth, in a manner even greater than what you had first envisioned. When attached to Me, you are available to bathe with Me in the channel of blessing that comes down from *Keter*, the highest *Sefirah* in which the whole world is sustained.

Why is it that I see *tzaddikim* with holy thoughts of building *yeshivos*, *cheders*, *mikvos* and other things, but their ideas never materialize? To my eyes, they suffer for years attempting to do the will of their Master and raise You back to your source, but to no avail.

My child, what you don't see is that, through their struggles, they have accomplished so much more than they would have if their plan was successful from the start.

How can that be, especially when, had their plan worked, many, perhaps hundreds, of Jews would have been helped, and many would have had their lives saved? To be honest with You, I too have plans in my heart but feel as if *HaShem* will not allow me success. I am not speaking of trivial matters, but very important projects. Those for which the world is starving and cannot wait even one more day without. There are poor people who must be fed - Jewish youth and others in the world who live in a time of spiritual famine. I'm prepared to be sacrificed in their stead, but *HaShem* is not allowing me to help them in the ways that I know.

Cry on this, my child. I see your heart yearns to give to another, but know that it is your broken heart that sustains Me this very moment. By doing so, you also give life to all those you wish to help. Therefore, your efforts and plans have not gone unanswered. It is sometimes the traveling and preparations for battle that win the war more than the actual battles. You have already done more than you realize. Happy are you for setting out on such a journey.

KABBALAS SHABBOS

Surely, I love praying the *Kabbalas Shabbos* prayers. I feel deeply moved by the *tefillos* and many times it sets the tone for my entire week. How does this event affect you?

My children, do you know how special *Kabbalas Shabbos* is? *Kabbalas Shabbos* is a very holy event, in many ways similar to a family reunion. *Kabbalas Shabbos* is for bringing a sense of unity amongst family and friends. It is a time of spiritual elevation for both mankind and the worlds above. It is an opportune time to elevate Me as I draw closer to you and your Father in heaven. The *Shabbos* has within it the hidden light of the world-to-come and its purity quenches the spiritual thirst of everyone. Welcoming the holy bride of *Shabbos*, bringing in *Kabbalas Shabbos* with joy, draws Me closer to the completeness I yearn for.

What meditations can I use to enhance my *Kabbalas Shabbos* experience?

During the first six prayers, you are elevating the six days of the week and binding them to the *Shabbos*. This is Myself escorting the *Shabbos* queen and she following Me down the aisle to the *chupah*. All around us are the holy *rabbaim* and their *chassidim*, followers basking in our light. Those who have sacrificed themselves to prepare for the *Shabbos* are following close behind the *kallah*, the *Shabbos* queen. Her dress is studded with pearls and sparkling diamonds. She wears ornaments you have placed upon her with your *Shabbos* preparations. If you have not prepared your home and self, it is difficult to see her and the beautiful clothing she wears.

If I have prepared for *Shabbos* with all my heart, tell me what I can see.

 Her light is shining. You cannot see her face, as it is covered under a veil. The holy *tzaddikim* are taking turns dancing before us as we walk. They are shining with joy. Groups of *rabbaim* with their followers are holding hands and rocking back and forth as we pass by. Even the simplest Jews dance before us, wishing to bring joy to their Creator. *Lecha Dodi* has already begun and the singing is beautiful. Those who know how, begin to meditate on the elevation process, *Yechudim* of the *Shechinah* and the Holy One blessed be He. The wish of every Jew is to be a part of this moment and to assist in My elevation. Even the simplest Jew praying these prayers is a part of this momentous elevation, and those in the lower heavenly worlds are raised as well.

 I and the princess begin to circle the *Keter* and the Throne of Glory seven times under the *chupah*. The *chasan* has waited all week for us. After each pass, I am raised up one more *Sefirah*, spiritual level. The *sheva brachos* then commence while you continue to sing *Lecha Dodi*. This is followed by the reading of the *kesubah*, and the words *bo-ee-v-shalom*. All turn around and reflect on the meaning of their lives while I am elevated and bask in wholeness. There is celebration in all the worlds and you generously escort us to the *yichud* room, singing the final *Lecha Dodi*. The Garden of Eden opens its doors and the greatest among the *tzaddikim*, beginning with the *Avos*, gather around us, singing and dancing. All of *Gan-Eden* leans over trying to get a glimpse of us and they are clapping, singing, dancing with great joy… Good *Shabbos*.

TORAH LISHMAH

Shechinah, **I have heard about the idea of Torah** ***lishmah*** **but, to be honest, I don't quite understand it.**
Well, what is your understanding of it?

I have heard from my study partners and friends that studying ***lishmah*** **means learning the Torah only in Hebrew or the original text. It is studying the Torah from the best of the** ***meforshim,*** **commentaries. Mainly,** ***lishmah*** **means studying the Gemarah and** ***halacha*** **meticulously. Is this a correct understanding?**
My child, your friends, may they be blessed, are misinformed. They do not understand what studying *lishmah* means. The idea of *lishmah* is a simple one. Any Jew can learn Torah *lishmah*, even those with the simplest backgrounds. It would not make sense for *HaShem* to make such an important concept complicated and inaccessible. The concept of Torah *lishmah* can be likened to the concept of faith; people philosophize about it and try to make it very complicated. Faith, like *lishmah*, is very simple.

Please tell me more.
HaShem doesn't care how great of a scholar you are nearly as much as He cares about the intentions you have in your heart while learning.

What should my intentions be while learning the Torah?
Simply to fulfill the *mitzvah* of studying Torah.

Are there other things I should have in my mind while studying?

Well, that is the main thing. One should learn how to perform the *mitzvah*, but not study in order to gain popularity or respect. You should have very pure intentions: To fulfill the *mitzvah* itself, nothing more. If you like, it is beneficial to have in mind the desire to bring happiness to *HaShem* by doing His will. Keep in mind that you are studying Torah *lishmah* in order to draw down *shefa*, blessing into the world. You may also bear in mind that you are studying in order to draw My presence upon you. When you have these thoughts in your mind, you will be happy. Your studying is pleasing both to *HaShem* and the entire world. Do not continue the misinformation. *Lishmah* is for all Jews in the world. It is studying *lishmah* that truly gives pleasure to *HaShem* and to our very own *neshamos*.

I have tried studying Torah *lishmah*, but I must admit that my intentions in studying have not been completely pure.

Even if your intentions are not pure, if you continue to study, eventually, your intentions will become pure. The Torah has the ability to heal a person's heart and desires. So don't give up and be persistent in doing the right thing because in the end, you will reach your objective.

COMING DOWN TO US

Shechinah, why is it that HaShem decided to extend Himself down to us?

The purpose of Creation was so *HaShem* could share the light of His greatness with other creatures. Since His full presence is too high and elevated for us to bear, He created Me, the *Shechinah*[2], to spread His light upon you in a more concealed way; one that wouldn't be too strong and destructive for a mere human being to handle.

Can Your light also be too strong for us?

You will feel only the amount of light and holiness that you, as a vessel, are able to handle. Certainly I could overwhelm you with My light, but I take great care not to. You are given just the right amount.

How do I help increase the amount of light I can receive from you?

More importantly is the fear of *HaShem*. Shlomo Hamelech said, "Fear of *HaShem* is the beginning of wisdom."[3] Just by pondering this a few moments, you will feel My presence. Should you think about it constantly, happy are you! How good is your portion! You will feel My light in your every limb. I will never leave your side.

---

[2] Not as a physical creation or actual being but an image of His holiness.

[3] Proverbs 1:7

What else will help me to feel your light?

You should yearn for My light to touch you. Pray to *HaShem* that My light is increased upon you. Cry out from the depths of your heart for your Mother to hold you. Don't forget Me during the night, when I too, am lonely.

Can I one day see a true vision of You?

It is possible. I will be dressed in black, a woman in mourning for the loss of her children, and like a widow separated from her husband.[4] It will be very difficult for you to bear seeing me this way, so you will have to work many years in preparation.

How much light is upon me at this moment?

Having separated your thoughts from the worldly, I am now right beside you; so close that if you close your eyes this very moment, you would feel Me holding you. I want to never let go of you, my child. Sin not, and I will remain with you forever. I will lift you up and carry you in My arms, like a newborn child all your days.

---

[4] It is known that some very holy sages were able to see this image at times. It is not a physical or created being but the essence of holiness.

ALONE AT NIGHT

Shechinah, why do You sit alone at night?
When night falls I am forced onto an unendurable path.

What kind of path are you forced to follow?
I am pulled by your many sins from world to world, lower and lower. Before each night I hope that *Klal Yisrael* will repent and I will not have to bear the horrible pain of the night.

We are sorry for having hurt You. We don't want to cause You pain, but only to reunite You with Your love.
That is what you always claim but in reality you don't care about Me. You constantly pull me further and further into impure realms, saying to yourself, "I will only commit a small sin and no one will see me."

We don't intend to hurt you. We care about you and can't stand to know you are trapped because of our sins.
If only you felt in your heart what you say with your lips, I would not be here.

Our hearts are broken, knowing what we did to you. Will you be able to forgive us?
You ask for forgiveness only to repeat the identical wrong again. Am I to forgive over and over as you push Me further and further from My love? Have you no heart that you trample all over Me? Do you get so much pleasure from doing evil actions that you simply forget about Me? Don't

you realize how much bad you create in the world by your repeated sins?

The pain I have caused You is not one that can heal in a moment. If only I could turn the clock backwards and take back my wrongs! Unfortunately, all I can do is move on from here. Will You try to forgive me even though it is hard for You?

Do you think I can bear a grudge against My children? I would place Myself in danger to protect you. I have gone down with you into exiles[5], intending to protect you. When I embrace you, how come you turn away?

When do you embrace me?

Every time you feel close to *HaShem*, it is I who stands next to you in a chariot to your Father. Your Father can't bear to look at Me when the children I bore[6] for Him turn against Him. Only when you do good deeds am I able to inch closer to Him. Even when We see each other from a distance, it gives Us pleasure, but when you sin, you cloud over the air and We separate.

---

5 Spiritually *HaShem* sent the *Shechinah*, sparks of His Essence to accompany us through the exile.

6 The *Shechinah* is compared to a mother. Though we are not physically birthed by her. The idea is used as an analogy of our relationship with *HaShem*.

EVIL THOUGHTS

***Shechinah*, what do I do? I feel like my thoughts are out of control.**

You must believe you can control them. *HaShem* would not give you even one thought that you can't fight off. Thoughts appear when a person is idle. If you get negative thoughts, distract yourself with chores and other things you must get done. For every negative thought, there is a positive one. You don't have to fight; simply switch channels.

You make it sound so simple, but we both know that it's not. If it were, the world would be a different place.

That is the problem with you, my children; you think everything is so complicated. I said it before and will say it again, serving *HaShem* is simple. Why do you make it so complicated? Our sages taught you plenty of ways to overcome bad thoughts and temptations. It all comes down to one thing, do you have the will to do it?

What You suggest sounds simple but for me it is a never-ending battle. I wish I could just simply flip a switch and redirect my thoughts. These thoughts control my life until they destroy every last ounce of my confidence.

Not only do I understand what you go through; I am even going through it with you. *HaShem* sent Me[7] to be with

---
[7] Not physically, the Shechinah is not physical or a living being. It is feeling the light of Hashem and His presence with a person.

you and that means if you go to the deepest depths I have to go with you. Can you imagine what that is like for Me?

Please; I do not wish to cause You pain and I don't want to continue these endless struggles. Teach me how to rise above them.

Do not take for granted what I told you. You must understand it. I will add more instructions that I hope will help you. The constant battle that you refer to has caused anger to build up inside of you. Instead of fearing only *HaShem*, you fear you struggles. You look upon yourself as weak and you are angry at yourself. Take this anger and use it to your advantage. Develop a hate for this evil. When you dislike something, even a simple food, there is no way you would allow yourself to eat it. The same thing here; if you teach yourself to dislike the taste of sin, and you hate that which tempts you to do such, it is more beneficial than anger at yourself. If he runs after you, let him see that this will only strengthen you to serve *HaShem* more. He will desist from bothering you, since it will serve no purpose. My children, understand that the *Satan* fights with a few guns and arrows, but you have the power to overcome him with great strength. The *Satan* is no match for the *Torah*. He may have grown stronger during this long exile, but when you look to *HaShem* for help by praying, learning the great Torah and gain advice from *gadolim*, you can prevail most certainly. Should you do so, you will be happy. The struggle will have been well worth the reward!

SLANDER/LOSHON HARA

Why is slander considered such a serious sin?

Every time you talk or think bad of another Jew, you are testifying against yourself and the person you are slandering, since all Jews are connected. But that is not all; your sins are now brought before *HaShem* to be judged.

What does this mean? How does it happen?

Before you spoke this forbidden slander, a few *malachim* wanted to prosecute you but were unable to bring judgement against you. When you spoke *loshon hara* it opened up their opportunity for judgement from Heaven; now *HaShem* will agree to view the full picture. Before, *HaShem* gave you the benefit of the doubt. Now that you spoke against a fellow Jew, *HaShem* is shocked and calls to the *Satan*: "Tell me what is going on with this fellow... He did what?" Immediate judgment is passed against the slanderer for all his bad actions. The slander might be a small part of the sin entourage, but it is the MAIN cause of punishment.

Could a sinful person walk through this world untouched if he does everything wrong but speak slander?

Most sinful people are not careful with their words, so it is unlikely to happen. Nevertheless, remember how terrible it is to think and speak badly of anyone. When we speak badly of people, we embarrass them in front of others and we could cause them to have a bad name for years to come.

What can I do to improve in the way I speak to others?
Think before you speak and don't say unnecessary words. Our *rabbaim* have said that one of the most beautiful things a person can do is to keep silent. People talk way too much about frivolous and meaningless things. It was the practice of great *rabbaim* to practice a *tannis debur*, where they would not talk for an entire day in order to purify their minds and speech. People talk so much sometimes, that they only confuse themselves and they can thereby make wrongful decisions.

What are some more benefits to being careful in this aspect?
Well if you don't speak badly about others, your friends will notice this, and they will feel like that can confide in you when they need too. A lot of time people talk badly because of pride. They think that putting others down will raise them up in front of their peers. Instead, they are only spreading hate with these actions and pushing themselves always from *HaShem*.

IS THERE PEACE?

Holy *Shechinah*, is there peace in the Heavens?
There is no peace in the Heavens right now. How can there be peace in the heavens when there is no unity among *Klal Yisrael*?

Is everything dependent on us?
When peace prevails among Jews the *Sefiros* above can flow freely between one another. When a *chasan* and *kallah* are married, peace comes to all the worlds. If it happens that someone is insulted on earth, yet keeps silent for the sake of peace, this makes a repair above. At this time there is too much hatred among our people. How can one Jew hate his fellow? Are you not part of one nation?

What can I do to increase peace in the worlds?
Smile… Do you know how much love and peace there is in a smile? Today no one makes a conscious effort to smile.

How should I converse with someone less religious than I am?
You can't change a person by making them feel bad about themself. We do this all too often, as it's difficult to know how to act when confronted with someone less religious. The best way is to show how Torah has made you a better person. Display your inner love for *HaShem* and the *mitzvos*, and remember that making a *kiddush HaShem* is the most important thing.

Please tell me more about the idea of peace.

Well there are many levels of peace. There is also a level of peace that a person must strive for internally. Many people are walking around with inner anger at themselves and with a low self-esteem. Just like one should try to have peace with other people, so too must they find an inner shalom and tranquility.

Thank You for drawing this to my attention as for years I haven't felt inner peace. So how do I reach this inner peace in my life?

Well, the first thing you can try is to find your good points. Don't dwell on negativity too long. The *rabbaim* say that a person who is a slave to their evil inclination does not have real peace in their life. So you must break free from the clutches of the *Satan* and then you will start appreciate the beauty of life.

HUGE STONE

Shechinah[8], I feel as if a huge stone has been placed right in my pathway. It is heavy, and its height reaches to the sky. What am I to do? I want to come close to *HaShem*? How do I continue without falling into the despair of evil?

My dear child, the *Yetzer Hara* might confuse you with the appearance of barriers but they are mere foolishness. You cannot be forced into evil.

I can understand this but still, the pathway to holiness is on the other side of this stone and I am on the wrong side.

Well my son, it's best not to touch it so don't climb over the top. Rather, go around it.

How am I to go around it? It is also very wide.

You must search deep inside yourself for this strength. It is there! *HaShem* does not give you an antagonist unless he also gives the weapons to defeat him.

Please shed some more light on me, as I have searched and don't see weapons strong enough for the army that attacks me.

---

8 The *Shechinah* is address sometimes through the holy name *Adna* and other names during prayers. This does not mean that we are praying to two separate G-d's. There is only One *Hashem* and the *Shechinah* is part of His light.

You have already been given right weapons you have been given; what you lack is a strong heart and will, and this is something you have to find in yourself. I believe you can if you truly want to.

I have the courage to fight but the enemy has already poisoned my mind with alien thoughts that go against Torah, confusing my thoughts. How am I supposed to win now?

If that is the case, stop thinking. Take the first step by separating yourself from the temptations and influences of the world, that you have become to accustomed to. Open up a *sefer* and begin to learn Torah. When *HaShem* created the *Yetzer Hara*, He also created its antidote, the Torah.

Thank you; I am less confused now. But back to this massive rock: I still must get around it. Which way do I go and how?

Always follow the path to the right. The path to the left is full of traps; you are sure to lose if you follow that way. As you take the right path, talk out to *HaShem* your worries and anxieties. Ask Him to help find your way around the rock. Search all the good points within yourself. Certainly you have accomplished great things in your life. You are gifted; you are a Jew. Temporarily occupy yourself with distracting things like music, reading, dancing, cooking, walking and the like so you can pass the time wisely. Before you know it, you will arrive on the other side of the stone. It wasn't as large as you thought. In fact, when you turn around to face it, you will notice that it disappeared. Was it really even there?

This is wonderful advice; I made it as You said. I also noticed that the stone was an illusion, but sometimes *HaShem* puts a real stone in front of you. When that happens, should I do anything different?

I guess you can say that these imaginary stones you face from time to time are a preparation for the real objects you will confront in your life. You should be thankful to *HaShem* that most of these are imaginary as if they were all real you would have done quite a bit of damage to your life in failing them from time to time. Know that even when you fail in some way you can still win if you have learned from the experience. Now that you know the secret that even in failure you can find the positive, there is no reason for you to ever become dejected and give up.

Tikkun Shechinah

MY CHILD

My child, have you forgotten the purpose of your existence? Has it been so long since you tasted the glory of the *Bais Hamikdash* that you care no more for her?

I have not forgotten that I am here to perform all of the *mitzvos* and to give *nachas* to the holy One blessed be His Name. Each night, upon my bed I cry and plead that *HaShem* return us to our home. This exile is so bitter. There is so much hate, so much pain. I cannot bear it much longer.

If this is how you feel my child, then why do you continue to destroy her? Don't you know that each generation that fails to rebuild the temple is counted to have destroyed it?

Every home is a small *Bais Hamikdash*. So many of us returned to the ways of our sages. Maybe You can see only the destruction we have caused; don't you see the good our generation has done?

Why take credit for *mitzvos* when that was what you were created to do? You perform a few positive *mitzvos* and continue to overlook so many. You shy away from the responsibility you have been given to change the world and fix yourself. Then you look to heaven for all of your materialistic desires and wonder why they are not fulfilled. Are you blinded by your physical body to such an extent that you cannot see Who it is that created you and for what Divine purpose you have been brought here for? Are you waiting until your soul feels so empty from your unworthy pursuits that suddenly you will be filled with repentance? Of course every good *mitzvah* you perform is seen and appreciated but so are your sins noticed. They are many and it makes little sense that someone who has been blessed with such a holy Jewish soul such as you continues to purposely push yourself further away from the truth.

You speak many words of truth and I value them sincerely. I hope to improve on my ways and use the blessing of life that I have been given in order to serve *HaShem* properly.

RESPECTING/TRUSTING TZADDIKIM

My child, why do you make light of the closest officials of the King of Kings, *HaShem* blessed be He?

The *tzaddikim* today don't seem to live up to the wonderful stories of *rabbaim* from previous generations. Whenever I choose a mentor, he seems to let me down.

You have to beg *HaShem* very hard to help you find and draw close to the *tzaddik* who will understand and help perfect your soul. It's not true that *rabbis* today don't live up to the levels they should. *HaShem* gives our generation exactly what you need and this *tzaddik* has it. If you were to resurrect the last generation of *tzaddikim* into our generation, aside from their greatness how would we understand each other? What would be the Arizal's reaction to your computer, cell phone, and camera? Would he allow you in his *Bais Midrash*?

So, if this is the case, I am still left in wonderment: How will I find the *tzaddik* for me or, if I have already found him, how can I draw more light from him?

Truth is something a person must constantly search for. A *tzaddik* personifies the idea of truth. You can always search for more truth, for a *tzaddik* attached to the root of truth, or for stronger attachment to the *tzaddik* you know. The benefit comes not necessarily from the *tzaddik* himself but rather the pathway to him.

How do I begin on this pathway?

Most importantly is to respect the sages. Do not underestimate the *tzaddikim* of your generation. Ask *HaShem* to draw you closer and to open your heart to receive from them. Respect their time but do not be afraid to tell them your needs. When immersed in the *mikvah*, in prayer or a *mitzvah*, say aloud and think to yourself that you are binding your *neshamah* to them. When properly attached to the *tzaddikim*, you will be surprised at the love and kindness they bestow upon you. You will finally see and appreciate the truth of the *tzaddik* and the *emes* for which the Torah stands.

HAPPINESS

Shechinah, **why is Your presence not upon me such as it was before?**

Before, I was with you because you had fear of *HaShem* and had a happy heart.

Why does my sadness cause You to depart from me?

It is not the sadness itself that chases me away but rather the sin that follows there-from.

You also mentioned a flaw in my fear of *HaShem*. How is this apparent to you?

When you lost happiness, you also lost a measure of belief in the oneness of *HaShem*. It is not that you purposely believed in multiple deities; rather, with a loss of hope, you simply lost your level of belief in *HaShem*.

Just because I occasionally stumble in my ways, should I be classed in the same category as non-believers?

If you are not believing and trusting in *HaShem* one hundred percent, then to a certain extent you are worshiping idols. How can you blame Me then for leaving you?

From what You have told me, I can see that if I guard myself from all unhappiness, it is certainly a foundation stone towards being a true servant of *HaShem*.

That is correct and that is why this simple emotion is a big target for the Evil Inclination. Depression can damage a person more than any one sin.

Tell me more about happiness and how it can affect me.

It is not just that happiness affects you alone but it also can lift up others around you. Joyousness is contagious and when a person is joyous, others want to be around them and enjoy this light, while sadness is an empty and lonely world that sinks a person to solitude. Happiness on the other hand can open so many positive doors in a person's life.

It sounds wonderful to be joyous all the time. I wonder why something so important and easy seems to be so difficult for so many people. So many people I know are anti-depressant medicines in order to stay happy. Why is sadness so prevalent today?

Really there is no secret pill to happiness. Being happy is a way of life and a person has to significantly change their perspective and how they live, think and go about their day in order to be a happy person. You have to be committed to happiness, and you must fight sadness as it is like a plague in our generation.

YOU FORGOT ME

For years you sacrificed your life, as it were, by arising at night to mourn over my solitude. My child, why did you draw close to me only to later forget my existence?

I didn't purposely stop my devotion to *HaShem* and the Temple. My situation changed. I saw no response to my cries, and so I decided to devote myself to other things.

What? Is this enough reason to turn your back on the wounded - that you saw no healing for your efforts? Is this a reason to stop giving support? I ask you: Did you really care to begin with?

Maybe not enough; I certainly wanted to be there for You and understand Your pain; I wanted the *geulah* and Your happiness; I wanted You to reunite with *Keter*[9].

You drew close to Me and then turned away; this caused me even more pain.

I didn't mean to make things worse. Please recall all the nights I cried for you and begged *HaShem* to take us all home.

I do remember. That is why I watch over you every day, and it pains me when you drift further and further from *HaShem*[10].

---

[9] In Kabbalah, the *Shechinah* is compared to *Malchus* and Her elevation is complete with *Keter*.

[10] The *Shechinah's* essence is there to help us draw closer to *HaShem*

You were there? Why didn't I feel You?

I hid Myself; it was important that you return to Me first, and now you have. If you will once again care for Me, I will be with you in a revealed state.

I will. I understand things much better now. That even when I don't feel You it is only because You wish to draw me close and are waiting for my soul to awaken. There is nothing more important to me than the redemption and holiness to prevail over the world. I'm sorry it took so long for me to awaken from this spiritual slumber. I will once again carry the burden of pains of the *Shechinah* upon myself and do everything within my abilities to elevate the world through *mitzvos*.

That is very sweet of you to say and know that My only desire is to draw you close. I wish only to nurture my holy children and together we can hasten the final redemption.

IMPROVING YOUR MEMORY

Shechinah[11], how can I improve the strength of my memory in learning Torah and in my general life?

When your mind is pure, you are able to search and recall information. When you are humble about your knowledge and strengths, your wisdom will be like a fully set table before you.

How is my spiritual purity connected to my ability to remember?

To understand this, you must understand your *neshamah*. At its source, the soul is a completely pure vessel, having learned all the Torah before birth. In previous incarnations, it performed many good actions and learned many wisdoms, but the soul forgets this holy information when attached to the physical body and its sins.

Is it true that *HaShem* purposely helps us forget?

Yes, *HaShem* understands that if you recall much of the good in your past, you will also recall the bad. Many would lose their minds from such an experience. So, do not believe that forgetfulness is all negative; it also benefits a person.

Are there any *segulos* I can do to help my memory?

---

11 The *Shechinah* is part of *HaShem's* Oneness and how He relates to His creations.

You can cook with olive oil. Also, only in clean places, picture the name of *HaShem YKVK*. Regular immersion in a *mikvah* purifies a person and so also improves the memory. Pray to *HaShem* to open your mind and heart to Torah. Should you follow My advice as in *Sefer Tikkun Shechinah*, with the wisdom of Torah, I will be with you and my presence will broaden your mind like the great sea.

Do the events and anxieties of my life have an effect on my memory?

Certainly they do. The great Rav Yochanan was having difficulty concentrating and his comrade Raish Lakish inquired as to why. Rav Yochanan explained that his money was recently stolen by people and therefore it was impairing his memory. A person can't study well while worried about *parnasa*.

The Horostyple Rebbe once responded to someone who asked him permission to study Torah all day and to rely upon faith alone for *parnasa*. The *rebbe* stated, "As long it doesn't give you anxiety, go ahead and do it." He was referring as You have spoken, to anxieties about money. Since yes, they do hamper one's concentration.

FINAL REDEMPTION

Shechinah, how close is Klal Yisrael to bringing the final redemption?

Galus has certainly been drawn out and difficult, but what keeps me together is how close the final redemption is at this time.

So, are You saying that I should expect Mashiach to come any day now?

Certainly, every day one should say the *Ani-maamin* prayer: I believe that the redemption can come today. You can expect the *Mashiach* to come but, more importantly, you should take the necessary steps to fulfill as many *mitzvos* as possible so the arrival of *Mashiach* will not be delayed.

What mitzvah should I work on to hasten the redemption?

It says in the Talmud: if the Jewish nation would keep *Shabbos* two times in a row, the *geulah* would arrive instantly. Why would the Talmud single out *Shabbos* and not keeping kosher or wearing *tefillin*? Let us ponder the qualities of *Shabbos* for a moment. What is *Shabbos*? It's a day of rest from the mundane and trivial pursuits of life. It's a time to focus on spirituality and the greatness of Torah, like the time of *geulah*. Through *Shabbos* observance we enter a form of redemption, because that is exactly what *Shabbos* is.

How am I to feel that the responsibility lies on my own shoulders?

For this reason our sages say: "Therefore every single person is obligated to say, 'The world was created for my sake.'"[12]

By doing so, he realizes that by helping others and nullifying himself, in the long run he truly ends up helping himself. This realization does not come overnight, and so we must regard the world selfishly at first and learn the hard way that blessing comes when we give to others, expecting nothing in return. Should one not regard the world as having been created for him, why would he take the responsibility for the world's rectification?

---

12 Mishnah Sanhedrin 4:5

THE SHECHINAHS HOME

There is a famous question that has been asked for ages: Should all Jews come and live in Israel before the *Mashiach's* coming? What do you think about this and how does it affect you?

Certainly it is a great thing for Jews to live in their homeland, where I dwell in My fullness[13]. If you want to come close to *HaShem* and feel My presence, there is nothing like it. If you wanted to witness an event, wouldn't you buy the closest seat you could afford?

I understand what You are saying, but are there some of us who shouldn't return home?

Would you buy front row seats for an event you didn't appreciate? It would be unfair to the performers and those fans who appreciate the event. If you are coming to Israel to sin and live a secular life, not only is it a chutzpa to me but you also ruin the event for everyone who came for the right reasons.

Do you want those who yearn to come close to *HaShem* and do *mitzvos* to come?

Yes, certainly. I want to be close to my children.

---

[13] The Talmud says that the *Shechinah's* presence is mainly felt in Israel.

So why are so many proper Jews not coming?

There are many people who need to live their lives outside of Israel to complete certain *mitzvos* and tasks for the good of their souls. At the same time, there are many who should return but choose not to. Many debate this question all the days of their lives, never to return and fulfill their lifelong dream.

What should these people have done differently?

They should have prayed and yearned to attain this. Didn't Moshe pray so hard to come to *Eretz Yisrael* that if he asked once more *HaShem* would have had to grant his wish? *HaShem* told Moshe, stop praying because if you continue then I will be forced to answer you and it is not you, but Yehoshua whose destiny it is to bring the children of Israel into *Eretz Yisrael*. Sometimes my friend, it isn't *HaShem's* desire for a soul to dwell in *Eretz Yisrael* so you shouldn't feel so bad. The yearning itself and the desire to acquire the *kedusha* itself is of great value. Through faith, a person acquires an aspect of *Eretz Yisrael*, it can be too such an extent that it is almost as if the person is here themselves. So strong is their longing for *mitzvos Eretz Yisrael* that their soul is enveloped in the inner aspect of *kedushas Eretz Yisael*. The prophets were not able to prophesize outside the land but if they had first come and remained a short time, they were able to continue prophesizing elsewhere. This is because *Eretz Yisrael* is acquired and a blessing. Once you have it, it may remain with you.

So how do I possess more of the *kedusha* of the land?

The aspects of prayer, faith and *Eretz Yisrael* go hand and hand. If you possess any of them, you also must thereby also share in the aspect[14] of the other concepts. It is also good to give charity and support those living in *Eretz Yisrael*. To

---

14 Likutey Moharan 7

own land is also very good. Believing in absolute faith in the coming of *Mashiach* and the return of all Jews to *Eretz Yisrael* is also fundamental.

HOLINESS IN SPEECH

My children, why do you talk and talk without counting and weighing each word beforehand?

As long as I am not cursing and hurting others, why should I count my words so carefully?

Each and every word that you speak has an effect on your *neshamah* for good or bad. When you talk idly, your talk having no purpose at that moment, you degrade me and your *neshamah*. Should you choose to speak holy words, you upraise and attach yourself to me. In fact through holy speech, you can bind to Me so strongly that we will be inseparable, since speech is attached to *Malchus,* and *Malchus* is attached to Me.

What about speech that is neither holy nor impure, such as in business?

This too you should attempt to elevate.

How do I do this?

When you talk about business or similar, focus your mind on the fear of *HaShem*. Fill your entire mind and body with this thought. Also, let your only purpose in speaking at this moment be to care for your physical needs quickly so you can return your thoughts entirely to *HaShem*.

Why did HaShem make speech so easy, and yet place within it so many foundations to holiness?

He wanted to make holiness and purity easily attainable for a person who truly desired it. Speech also has the power to easily destroy a person's soul.

Its power for both good and bad we seem to ignore.
This is so true; should you count and weigh your words, happy you will be. How pure you will become; I will always be with you and even your speech will radiate My light.

EATING WITH THE SHECHINAH

***Shechinah*, I heard that I can draw close to you through eating. Please explain how I can do this.**
Much of it depends on your intentions for the beginning and concluding blessings. If you eat for the proper reasons, the sparks in the food are elevated and my presence comes upon you.

What else should I do while eating?
It is important to chew your food well and not in a rushed manner. This will help to channel the food through the body in the proper way. It also helps to elevate the sparks and even you. It is certainly not beneficial to gobble down food in the same way an animal would.

What happens to me if I fail to follow this advice?
Instead of elevating the food to a human level, you degrade yourself, from man to animal.

What loss does the animal incur?
Here it has waited so long and undergone so much humiliation only to be elevated by you, and now it must undergo the same humiliation all over again. You have failed it.

What damage has been done to me?
Instead of a spiritual elevation after eating, negative sparks could enter your body and cause spiritual damage. This is why it is so important to concentrate your attention

throughout the entire eating process, from the first blessing until the concluding one. When you focus on the enjoyment and physical benefits of eating, you fail to take seriously its spiritual importance. When you focus on the spiritual, you can attain more spiritual revelations then you can imagine. Happy will you be and how strong your soul will become.

What else can I do to maximize the benefits of eating?

People are so careful to say the blessing before eating but many times forget the after-blessing which is a biblical ordinance. Be sure to not skip over this important *mitzvah*, and thereby, you will ensure that the food is properly elevated. Let us say for example that a person is given a book as a gift. He first thanks his friend for bestowing this kindness, and then he reads the book and benefits from it. Isn't it more proper to thank the person after you have benefited from the gift, than before? At first you're just giving gratitude in order to be polite but after the book changes something inside you for your benefit, certainly you should return this appreciation even more so. So too, after you have filled your stomach to your heart's content, it is only reasonable that you pay even more attention now than before to thank your host and He who has given you so much.

ONE'S LIVELIHOOD

***Shechinah*, why do so many suffer from week to week to support themselves?**

Worry over *parnasa* is one of the greatest purifications known to man.

If it is so purifying, how come the Gemara says that a poor man is like one who is dead?[15]

Yes, poverty certainly stills man's heart but it also does good. A dead man is humble and can't possibly suffer from pride or preoccupation with care of needless possessions. He has no choice but to place his trust in *HaShem*, as man has already failed him.

Maybe this is so, but most truly poor people I see are frail and full of depression and sorrow.

This is because they fail to accept their lot and be happy with life's important aspects, which they more than anyone should recognize. When they do, their strength and happiness are restored.

How can the poor man exchange his lot for a more stable one?

He should accept and be happy that *HaShem* knows what is best for him. He should place his trust on *HaShem's* shoulders, as it were, and increase each day his allotted time for prayer and meditation.

---

15 Talmud Nedarim 64

Should the poor man increase his load of work?

This can only be known on an individual basis. Many dismiss their responsibilities due to laziness and hide in an unreal faith. Some enter the house of Torah learning only to live in idleness and vanity. I ask you My children, be real with *HaShem* and yourself. Should you ask a winemaker to pour wine when you haven't given him a bottle to fill? If you don't work, you must learn Torah in earnest. If you are learning, you still have to give the winemaker a bottle to fill for you. Each man should do some form of work in his life. This curse was given to all men; why should you assume you are excluded and different? On the other hand, nobody said work should consume your life. Just give *HaShem* a bottle to fill and you can even spend most of your days in the house of study.

What about the stories in the Gemara that tell of Rebbe Shimon Bar Yochai studying Torah all day without being bothered to work?[16]

Reb Shimon was different; he was the actual bottle to fill as he was *shalaim*, complete and whole in his *midos*. He worked on his self-character to such an extent that he was never *bittle* Torah. Through this, he became a man of perfect faith. A man of perfect faith, a *tzaddik*, to him the *mana* in the desert came directly to his door and in an already prepared state.

Can I too reach this level?

Through hard work and toil, there is nothing beyond your grasp. For most though, making a physical vessel for *HaShem* to bless, will lead them to less *bitul* Torah. People in this generation have the tendency to become very idle with their time. Therefore, it is recommended they have what to fill in their day... not to mention, the *tikkun* of Adam and

---

16 Talmud, Tractate Brachos 35b

work is not a small matter. Be happy in your labors because through them, you can come to be honest in your partnerships and with others.

YOMIM TOVIM, A great time!

Shechinah, what is your connection with the _Yomim Tovim_, holidays?

These are days I strongly connect with my children, young and old; times full of joy and unity for all the right reasons.

So, is this a good time to get to know You?

Yes, it certainly is. Should you apply yourself during these times, I can reveal Myself strongly to you. I can lift you to heights of _devekus_, attachment, you never knew before.

How do I receive the greatest benefit from a _Yom Tov_?

Prepare yourself by learning the _halacha_ and _sode_, the mystical reasons for the holiday. This way you will enter _Yom Tov_ with the awareness needed to perform the commandments of the moment to the highest extent, with no need to interrupt your focus.

Please; if there is additional light You can shed on this matter, I will cherish it?

Okay, since you asked further, I will tell you: Do not underestimate even the simplest customs and smallest details demanded on this day. In one detail you may overlook a spiritual light so bright that, should you pay close attention, can elevate your soul to a level of _bitul_ in the light of _HaShem_.

What else can You share with me that would help me enjoy these special days?

The main thing is to have joy and to share this joy with others. It is the joy of performing *mitzvos* and sharing this joy with others that makes the holiday great. Bringing people together to rejoice in *HaShem* and His commandments is everything. Prepare vigorously your home and food so that everyone has the maximum enjoyment of both body and soul. The effort you put into something, makes the reward all more enjoyable, but don't get carried away either and loose site of this great opportunity to study Torah with an open mind embracing the extra holiness of your *Yom Tov* soul.

SPIRITUALITY OF MUSIC

I would like to appreciate the spiritual benefits and aspects of music. Can You assist me in this?

The spiritual power of music is so great that the prophets entered all the gates of heaven with music as their tool, climbing it like a ladder passing each octave. The sounds they made came alive inside them, rumbling gracefully through their nervous systems. Once at the top, they would become *bitul* in the lights of *kedusha*.

What type of music is most beneficial for this?

Devekus nigunim from holy *tzaddikim*; many were written with this intention in mind. There are differing traditions whether to use Jewish music with or without *pesukim*. Some feel that words interfere with the elevation, while others believe it enhances the experience. One has to discover a way that works best for him.

How are You related to this experience and to the power of music?

The purpose of music is the joy it radiates into a person; music makes a joyous heart. You can't receive spiritual revelations without a joyous heart. You would be immediately turned away and thrown down from your place. As soon as you are joyous, my presence immediately rests upon you.

Is it better for one to be his own musician to reach spiritual heights through it?

It is not necessary, but there are advantages. The actual striking of keys or strings can be its own meditation. Singing can also be very meditative but, for some, just listening to music is sufficient; then one doesn't have to be preoccupied with the notes he must play correctly. Again, in this aspect, you should find your own way. If you're going to listen to music played by others, make sure that the lyrics are in holiness and that the musician himself has pure intentions. The music a person listens too has the ability to draw him either closer to holiness or *chas-v-shalom* to the side of unholiness. So make sure you select the type with caution.

Tikkun Shechinah

DON'T TRAVEL WITHOUT ME

Why should I make sure that I travel with You?
My presence is a protecting One. Should it be upon you, it is rare that you will ever get hurt and all your doings are surer to go smoothly. Should I let go of you, or you of Me, you are open to the world and its trivial happenings. I protect you from all dangers and evils.

This is truly amazing; I didn't realize the magnitude of strength and protection you give. Now that I know this, how can I ever purposely let go of you?
It was the way of Dovid Hamelech to never let go of me. The *Satan* was unable to take his life so he made a noise to disrupt his attachment for but a moment and it was that second he left this world.[17]

Do people attach themselves to You like they did in Dovid Hamelech's time?
Even several hundred years ago, the simple Jew thought about Me and meditated on this attachment. Today, few even try. Should they do so, rarely do they even recognize the validity of their attachment. Nonetheless, I am still there to protect them. I just wished they knew Me as one would know the mother who gave birth to them.

This is very sad but honestly, many of us simply do not know how to relate to You.

---

17 Talmud Shabbos 30

Please my children; let us get to know one another. Why should we have to suffer the pains of this *galus* alone when together we can bring each other comfort? The first step in relating to Me is to realize My importance. Then, purify yourself and begin making an attachment. Next, learn how to sustain this connection. Eventually the attachment will grow and grow and the benefits will be everlasting.

So, how can I connect to You more often?

When you learn Torah and do *mitzvos*, you connect to me. When you never stop thinking about *HaShem*, and you recognize Him in all aspects of your life, the *Shechinah* will be there.

TZITZIS

Shechinah, can you tell me about the *mitzvah* of *tzitzis*?
We spoke previously about taking great light and lowering it to the common people. *Tzitzis* more than almost any *mitzvah* lowers itself to the bottom realms just to bring holiness upon a person. A person can wear *tzitzis* while in the bathroom and in many situations you could normally not perform a *mitzvah*.

If it can go down to such levels, shouldn't I assume it can't at the same time be very high?
It's the opposite of how it might appear to you because it can go so low, that is exactly why it must be so high.

Can you explain this to me as maybe I can learn some important lessons from this?
Well, the entire greatness of something high is that it affects that which is low. The *tzitzis* do just this; they are high and they have a great effect on the low.

How can I fulfill this *mitzvah* in the best way so as to bring out its greatness?
Its strength begins when you say the blessing for it upon arising. Should you say it with all your heart, you will draw its protective light upon you. It is important to look upon it occasionally throughout the day with respect, and reflect how it contains all the 613 lights of the

commandments. Wearing the *tzitzis* so that the strings are visible helps in this aspect.

What other benefits are there?

If you fulfill the *mitzvah* of *tzitzis* properly, your purity, concentration in prayer and *paransa* will increase drastically. As said before, the main time to make the *kavanah* is when you put on the *tzitzis* garment in the morning. At that time, pour out your heart to *HaShem*.

SWEETENING JUDGMENT

Shechinah, how can I sweeten the judgment already passed in Heaven?

It is good to reflect every night, before retiring to sleep, on the deeds you performed that day. This way, you cancel the future judgment that had yet to take place and sweeten that which already had passed.

What if I forget to do this? What else can I do to help myself and others?

If you care for your soul, you would not take the above statements lightly. This practice can not only save your life but it also gives life. You should not and cannot truly live without utilizing this lesson. Ignoring it and not installing it into your nightly routine is foolishness.

Thank You for bringing this to my attention. I have tried it a few times but after a while I discarded this teaching.

That only proves its worth, that you so easily forget and ignore it. You asked Me what else you could do to help sweeten judgment. I recommend praying often, specifically reciting *tehillim*. Charity will save a person from near death, how much more it should help with smaller things. One important factor is to judge all people on the side of merit. There is a famous teaching from our sages that *HaShem* tests a person by first letting him judge his friend in what will soon happen in his life also. If he judges his friend towards the side of merit, then *HaShem* will too. Should he judge his friend sternly, so in his time will *HaShem*. To be honest with you, this teaching is a very gentle way of laying this idea upon you.

Please explain to me why you feel it is so gentle.

My child, all of your spiritual strength, insights and self-growth, stem from trying to find the merit in another. How can *HaShem* not judge such a person on the side of merit who finds no fault in another? One who acts in this way is given special *hatzlacha* in heaven and will succeed in all he does.

PERFECT SIMPLICITY

Shechinah, I have heard that serving *HaShem* in the ways of simplicity can be greater than serving with sophistication. Can You explain this to me, as it doesn't seem logical?

Sophistication appears to the human eye as wise and a prerequisite to greatness. To spiritual eyes and the eyes of *HaShem*, this is not so. Sophistication leads to self-gratification and pride. These are things that draw a person far from the truth and *HaShem*.

How can I know which stringencies to take upon myself and if they will lead me closer to *HaShem*?

It takes a great deal of reflection and observation. You have to look deeply into your life and your *mitzvah* observance to see if it is real.

Please explain more to me how to tell if my practice is real and simple.

If you find you have added so much that you are not following the basic *halacha* and commandment itself, you need to re-evaluate. Should you see that *mitzvah* observance is causing you or your family stress, do some reflection.

So, is it a good or bad thing to add *hanhagos* into one's life?

If you are going to add *hanhagos* and *minhagim*, try to make sure you are doing it *lishmah*. It certainly can be beneficial to add to your service of *HaShem*; it's just that you have to make sure you are adding and not subtracting. It's easy to fool yourself.

When I watch *tzaddikim*, they appear to me very sophisticated, having taken upon themselves many *hanhagos*.

I leave you with this thought, for in it are many secrets about simplicity. If you would speak more to the *tzaddikim*, you would realize that to you what is sophisticated is to them simple.

LAZINESS

My child, why do you go about your days being lazy? Do you not understand that this world is a temporary one?

I feel a need to relax from all the stress of my day to day work.

My son, you seem focused more on relaxation than *avodas HaShem*. In the next world, you will have all the time you desire for relaxation. This world is a passing one; if you don't grab all you can, the opportunity will be lost. Connecting to *HaShem*, basking in His light, this is true bliss and relaxation. You try to calm your mind with materialistic solutions, but they only cause you more confusion. The greatest peace is reuniting with the source from where you came, the light of *HaShem*.

What You said makes so much sense.

Can you imagine the person who constantly says, "I want to learn such and such a craft?" But when the opportunity arises for him to study it, he doesn't show up, arrives late or doesn't pay attention during class. This is how you presently serve *HaShem*. You say you are lovesick to draw close to Him, yet you constantly tarry in your service. If you would take *avodas HaShem* more seriously, He in turn would accept your prayers and petitions with a more serious response.

You're correct and I will work on this aspect; please go on.

Laziness and idleness only lead a person in one direction and that is to sin. On the other hand, staying focused and organizing your time leads to *mitzvos* and accomplishments. When you are completely devoted to *HaShem* and you are using every moment for Him, He will place before you opportunities you may otherwise not see. Not only will you be above laziness, but you also may be above time.

HOLINESS OF TEFILLIN

***Shechinah*, can You tell me about the *mitzvah* of *tefillin*?**
    Usually when you have something valuable, you put it in a special safe to protect it. In the case of *tefillin*, even the *batim* are similar to a safe and must be protected as they too are valuable.

Please explain to me its value.
    Its value is more precious than pearls, more valuable than the rarest diamonds. Should it not have been made exactly as told by our sages, its value is diminished greatly and it can even become *posul*. For instance, the boxes have to be perfectly square and painted black. The ingredients for making the *batim* have no intrinsic value but, when put together, they become alive and radiate light.

What about the *parshios*? What value do they have?
    It is said that the intentions the *sofer* has while writing affects a person greatly. Also, each time a person puts on the *tefillin*, the *bracha* and respect he treats them with build and so does the *tefillin's* holiness. It is very important to never talk idly while wearing them.

Are the straps important?
    Yes, they are a *halacha* given to us by Moshe Rabbenu on *Har Sinai*. They must be black and made from special materials. The arm straps are wrapped around your arm seven times to represent the drawing down of the seven *Sefiros*. The straps on the head are wound to spell out *Shakai*, the holy

name of *HaShem*. When you wear *tefillin*, you are bringing down light from above and surrounding yourself with it.

What meditations should I have while wearing them?

There are countless things you should think about. The main thing to meditate about is fear of *HaShem*. The head *tefillin* have four compartments representing the holy name *YKVK*. Thinking of this brings a person to fear the One above. Just as the writing on the tablets were in black fire on white fire, so too are the *parshios* of the *tefillin*. The straps are also filled in black fire. So have in mind that you have surrounded yourself with the light of *kedusha*.

CHESED

***Shechinah*, in what way does doing kindness affect a person?**

Kindness very much molds a person into a true *ben* or *bas* Torah. It brings a person to very high levels of humility and it not only gives life to the person you help but yourself as well.

What weight does the *mitzvah* of *chesed* hold during *HaShem's* final evaluation of a person after they leave this world?

The sages tell you that doing *chesed* is so important that a person should put aside his Torah learning if no one else is available to help. That is certainly a lot of weight, as learning Torah is equal to all the *mitzvos* combined; to stop it in order to do kindness shows us many things. In certain situations, it can be higher than learning Torah and if that is the case, then *chesed* has the power to lift you up spiritually to the highest of levels.

That is certainly remarkable. Tell me more what *chesed* does for my *neshamah*.

Part of learning Torah is actually performing that which you study. The Torah teaches us how to look above ourselves and how to give to others, not only physically but also spiritually. If while doing the *chesed* you really would rather be somewhere else then you are helping but not wholeheartedly. You may think you are really giving to another but you could also be robbing them. When you give wholeheartedly with a smile, you give much more. Your *mitzvah* is genuine. You have elevated yourself and another.

There are many types of *chesed*; how do I know which one to take upon myself?

It all depends on the needs of those around you and your personal expertise. For instance, someone with a strong personality would be good at a *chesed* involving people. It would be best to do something kind with the talents *HaShem* has blessed you with. Doing *chesed* elevates a person to new heights. Should you find yourself not doing much *chesed*, it's time to re-evaluate your approach to Torah learning, as you have missed an important ingredient of a Torah life.

BRINGING A FINAL PEACE

Shechinah, why is peace such an important pursuit and why does it affect You so much?

The entire reason for this *galus* is in order to properly restore peace to the physical and spiritual realms. By there not being peace in the heavens I am not at peace, as the pathway to me is fractured. Your job is to restore peace in all the worlds.

How do I do that? It sounds like a tremendous undertaking.

It most certainly is and that is why the *galus* has been for so long. Fortunately though, most of the broken vessels are repaired and only a few remain to be fixed.

That sounds wonderful; I didn't realize we were so close to redemption. What can we do to finalize everything?

Do as many acts of kindness and *mitzvos* as possible. Never underestimate the power of a single *mitzvah*. Treat every person as you would want yourself to be treated. Say or have in mind before performing a *mitzvah*, "I am doing this in order to elevate the *Shechinah* to the Holy One blessed be He." This will help raise Me and that elevation will repair those final pieces bringing peace to the heavens.

Is there anything else I should know that will assist me in this important task?

If there is no peace below, there is no peace above. Even a simple feud with a friend or spouse separates the heavenly spheres from perfection. Be wise my son. The greatest peace is one between opposites and enemies. Only a humble person wants and runs after peace.

I wish I felt more peace in my life; it seems that I never have peace-of-mind.

Besides establishing a peace with others, one has to find an inner peace within themselves. It is important to understand who you are and where you are truly holding in life. People try to fill this empty feeling they have with materialistic solutions only to find that they give no lasting peace. A person who is at peace with themselves is someone who is no longer controlled by their evil inclination. It is someone that can look into the mirror at the end of the day and say to themselves, "I gave it my all. I did my very best today."

SHIDDUCHIM

Shechinah, what can I do in order to bring my _bashert_ sooner?

The most important thing is to have _emunah_ in _HaShem_. It was He Whom created two souls together as one, and He separated them, and only He can reunite them.

What are your feelings about _shadchanim_ and other matchmaking services?

The best thing is to have people who know you well searching for you. Nothing beats a real friend or _rabbi_ looking out for you. _Shadchanim_, it is a great thing that they share with you their precious time which they could instead share with their family. When you meet a matchmaker, it is important that you are confident in yourself. You should know in which direction you are going in life. There should be _rabbis_; friends, _yeshivos_, seminaries and whatever support groups you can build for yourself. Try not to take offense at the words of a _shadchan_. At times he may cause you emotional pain, but know that this is from _HaShem_, even though it may seem false and unjustified. _Shachanim_ should try to be very sensitive to singles, who are painfully alone. Should you have previously chosen a _rabbi_, a spiritual _derech_ and a physical one, it will make your matchmaking encounters smoother. It takes a special person to be a _shadchan_ and you must try to show appreciation and patience. Sometimes the person you least expect becomes your messenger. Still, don't place your hope and trust in man.[18] Place it in the hands of the King of Kings, *HaShem* blessed be He.

How can I ready myself to receive my intended partner?

Many get offended when they are told they must work on themselves, but isn't that what the whole idea of *bashert* is intended to accomplish? It is to complete oneself as a person! Even after you are married, you still have to work on making a real partnership. So my recommendation is to work very hard on your purity. If you are impure in your thoughts and actions, especially with the opposite gender, this distances you from your real intended partner. When you purify your heart and mind, trusting in *HaShem*, your *bashert* draws closer. Pray and beseech *HaShem* to save you from your loneliness. I usually rest with those who are married[19], but that is not to say the *Shechinah* cannot rest upon those who are single. I most certainly can and it would be My greatest pleasure to be with you. You must not think you're alone, since you haven't found your *bashert*. I can fill much of your loneliness and heartache. Call to Me, think of Me, bind yourself to Me and I will be to you a gracious Mother bestowing upon you blessing and wholeness.

I certainly would like to bond myself to You; I can't bear my loneliness alone.

One other thing I can recommend to you: Do not be too quick to judge a possible partner. You know, one reason why *HaShem* may withhold your intended one is the fear that you will only see faults and turn down the match. Therefore, He waits till a person can see for himself the type of match he needs. If you are open-minded at the start, you may save years of aggravation. Doesn't *HaShem* want to bring your

---

18 Psalms 20:8

19 Sota 17a

bashert today? Review with those wiser than you: What is most important to be looking for in a match? Be patient with people; give others a chance just as you would like someone to give you.

How do *shidduchim* today differ from those centuries ago?

The Talmud says that making a match is like the splitting of the sea[20], today, making a match has become as difficult as splitting the ocean. Today singles are coming from so many different walks of life. Due to technology, people are exposed to more things both good and bad. Many are emotionally off balance and carry much pain inside. It is important to try and really understand those you are matched up with. Place your trust in *HaShem* and the two of you will soon be one. May *HaShem* help you grow to the level you need for meeting your *bashert* easily.

---

20 Talmud, Sotah 2a

BENIFITS OF HALACHA

Shechinah, can You open my eyes into the importance and specialness of learning and following _halacha_.

    A person's first observation of *halachos* is that they have little spiritual essence and add pressure upon a person's life. My children, this is a mistaken understanding; the *halachos* are physical doors into the spiritual realms. When someone follows a *halacha*, I become attached to that person. The wick of the candle is prepared; all that is left is to light it with your heart.

What exactly is a _halacha_?

    A *halacha* is a guide and tool our sages gave to help a person follow the paths that lead a person close to *HaShem* and spiritual perfection. Without them it is like traveling through a mountainous desert with no map; you will certainly get lost and circle around your already trodden paths.

How do You recommend I learn the _halachos_?

    The proper way is to first see inside the *halacha's* source, the Chumash, Mishna, and then Gemara. Study it and then search through Rashi and Tosfos; the Rosh, Rif, Ran and the Tur Shulchan Oruch. It is also proper to learn the Chafez Chaim's Mishnah Berurah or to seek the final *halacha* from your Rav.

That sounds like an endless road of perusal. I barely know the basics.

First study either the Kitzur Shulchan Aruch or the Chai Adam and know it well. Afterwards, read many of the contemporary sage's books on how to live your life according to *halacha*, but to truly understand halacha and know it well, there is no escaping the Gemara.

Sometimes I find learning *halacha* to be taxing, boring and very pressured.

I understand you like to learn the stories of the Talmud and enjoyable works. However, once you get used to the format of learning *halacha*, it too is just as enjoyable. You will find that understanding *halacha* is the key to the beauty of the *hagadata* of the Gemarah. Once you have the stories and the *halachos* together, that is when the Torah becomes more open to you. It is true, you gain fear of *HaShem* through the study of *halacha* but stories contain both love and fear together. They also help to sink into your mind the *halachos*. That is why Talmud Bavli is so full of stories, it is because the *rabbaim* of the later generation understood that a good surrounding story to a difficult *halacha* will sweeten it. The Yerushalmi's didn't need these extra stories in order to follow the laws, they were stronger in their *avodas HaShem*, not to falter to the left or right.

What can I say, I am scared to learn more *halachos* as then I will have more responsibility to follow them all.

Is that an excuse not to study? You will follow what you can, and *HaShem* will give you the strength you need to keep the Torah. People assume that life is more difficult as you become more religious but it's actually the reverse. The more you add to your service of *HaShem*, the easier life is. Without following *halachos*, your mind is filled with worries and fears. When you follow the *halachos*, you only fear *HaShem* and you don't worry about needless things. Life becomes simpler and far less difficult.

ANGER

My children, why do you fall into obvious negative traits like anger? Don't you realize the damage you cause to your soul?

When I get angry, it happens very quickly, I do not have time to prevent it. What do you recommend I do to control it?

Kiss the *mezuzah* when you walk in and out of rooms. Immediately when you feel anger bursting inside you, occupy yourself with something else, change your surroundings. You might make for yourself a certain system; for instance, take a glass jar and drop a marble into it each time you feel angry. Listen to it bounce onto the bottom of the jar. Let this be your anger. Drop another if you need to. The goal of this exercise is to help you think first before you react. With ease, you will soon not need any assistance.

Please continue to shed light on this subject.

Well, to be upfront with you, many excuse themselves and think they do not have a problem with this *midda*, while inside they are bursting with built-up anger. Be truthful with yourself. Sometimes you might need to express your angry thoughts to *HaShem* or a close friend. Don't live your life full of tension. You may think your friend doesn't realize you are angry at him but usually someone is able to sense another's tension.

I do feel that I have anger built up inside me, but I have always assumed it is better held within.

    In many cases, inside anger can do far more damage than exterior anger. Not only do you hurt your soul, but you also bring harsh judgment upon yourself and the other person. You may think you are not hurting him but you most certainly are. A person would have to be extremely well mannered not to let on that he is angry, but you cannot hide your anger from *HaShem*.

How does my anger affect my relationship with you?

    The moment you become angry, I am gone. You are on completely on your own. I cannot bear to watch you tear up your soul and forget about before Whom you stand. *HaShem* says, "I, and he who is angry cannot be together." Therefore, when you become angry, you are in serious danger. You should immediately find refuge in the Torah and that which it stands for. Pray constantly to *HaShem* to rid you of this trait and you will succeed.

CHANNELS OF BLESSING

***Shechinah,* how can I ensure that blessing will descend on me without being blocked?**

You should always make sure that your sins are before you. It is also important to make sure you have inner peace. Your character traits should be balanced and your intentions and heart you should strive to make pure.

Is it true that I am a microcosm of the spiritual realms?

Every limb of your body has its reflection above and was created parallel to different spiritual aspects.

How is my life affected by the flow of both spiritual and physical life-forces?

Well, physically blood is flowing from one limb to the next and when one part is severed with a defect or illness, the blood flow to that area has to change and this change affects all the limbs that the blood has to flow to thereafter. Each sin we commit has a certain limb that it affects both physically and spiritually. It therefore clogs up the path of the blood in this area or spiritually it blocks the power and strength of that limb's spiritual counterpart.

Should I assume that this is the reason many things in my life seem to be going awry?

Let me ask you my child, do you feel the channels of blessing are flowing to you without veering off in another direction?

I do feel blessing descending upon me. It's just that I feel there is more that should come my way for the use of good in my life and it is not. What can I do about this?

Examine your ways to ensure you are truly doing the best you can. Ask yourself, am I helping others to my full capacity? Am I making good use of my time and strengths? Have I left the ways of sin and chosen fully the path of righteousness? Do I believe totally in *HaShem*?

My child, as we speak, the channels are already descending more gracefully throughout your body and soul. Continue on this path of reflection and on how good your lot will be. *HaShem* has so much he wants to give you that to date he was forced to withhold. It now depends on you!

HOSPITALITY

Shechinah, how important is it to be hospitable?
It is very important and can bring a tremendous amount of light and sustenance into one's home.

I find that it can bring much pressure and stress upon our family to have guests, so I tend to shy away from it.
Having guests and serving them brings renewal to one's family. If I was previously forced to leave, I return to your home when you courteously care for your guests.

Please tell me more about this important *mitzvah*.
When you have a guest, you provide for them lodging, food and countless life-giving materials. They become dependent on you for this sustenance; therefore, you give them life. When *HaShem* sees this, He in turn gives you life. Happy is the person who opens his home to others!

What else can I do to exemplify this *mitzvah*?
Well the most difficult thing for a guest is being comfortable and feeling like they are in their own home. Do your best to take this awkward feeling away from them and help them to feel at ease. This *mitzvah* is so great because even the strongest of men feel fatigue and anxieties from traveling. They never know what new event or delay they will encounter. When you take some of this discomfort away, you leave upon them a lasting memory of gratefulness. You have done them a great pleasure and they will not forget this easily. Even Avraham got out of his sick bed to look for guests

because he understood they if he doesn't help the traveler, nobody else would. They do not have the luxury of asking friends or family to assist them. Rather they are in un-trodden territories and in some cases, the discomfort of travel can be torturous. This is why this *mitzvah* is so special. A sick person, it is obvious you need to help him but a wary traveler, who thinks of him?

WORRIES OF THE HEART

Why is it that, when I worry about matters in my life, your presence seems absent from me?

A person worries because he doesn't trust that *HaShem* will send him salvation. If your trust was full, why would you suffer anxieties of the heart?

So, what should I do to strengthen myself when I suddenly feel anxiety?

Think about *HaShem*, how He has always cared for you; that the keys of salvation are only in His hands and He will send you relief very soon. Many times this takes place the moment your heart returns to Him, lifting the anxieties off your shoulders and placing them on His.

Why does *HaShem* allow a person something to worry about in his life? If I were to sit here a few minutes and think of things I could easily worry about, the list would be unending.

This is true; you should give yourself credit for having placed these matters in the hands of *HaShem* to solve. Many times, He is the only one who can solve them; the worries were sent to you only so you should lift the *Shechinah* back to its source.

Sometimes I wonder why my salvation doesn't come immediately.

HaShem certainly is patient with you, waiting sometimes years for you to repent over even a small matter.

Shouldn't you also be patient with Him? If salvation has not come yet, there is good reason for it that only He knows. So cast your worries and anxieties on Him and be strong, my child.

I have done my best to follow Your advice, but I still suffer from panic attacks and anxieties. What should I do?

You have to train yourself to accept that you're not in complete control of how you feel and of everything that happens in the world and that this is okay. People who think they are in control of everything are the ones that have no control. You who are searching for control at least are trying to fix yourself to have more faith in *HaShem*. What you must understand is that you are in control of one important aspect. That is, how you're going to act when you have anxiety and panics. Having anxiety is fine, everyone gets these feelings in different strengths. The wise one is the one who preservers through with faith and holds onto his faith the best he can. Soon after, the anxiety will disappear. Avoiding anxiety, is actually forcing more anxiety. Nothing is ever as bad as it first seems. There is always hope.

WOMEN & THE SHECHINAH

I have heard before that women represent the *Shechinah*; how am I to understand this?

It could be understood[21] that I am the feminine aspect of the *Sefiros*, the *Malchus*, receiving light from the *Keter*, the male aspect of the *Sefiros*. Why are we compared to both? Because the *Keter*, male, is the giver and *Malchus*, the female, the receiver. In this same way, I am the vessel receiving the higher light and completing the task of descending to the lower worlds, like a woman who brings completeness to her home and her husband.

Can you explain this to me with more practical examples?

Malchus is a reflection of *Keter*. A woman is a reflection of her spouse. When he blocks the channel of light to her through sin, depression, anger and pride, there is little light sustaining her. The peace and connection between them is broken. I also depart from them since, in the spiritual realms, they have also blocked the light from coming to Me. I also am caused to suffer.

How is a woman able to relate to You?

She should yearn to bring completeness to her home and the entire world. This is her strength. In her hands are

---

21 The *Shechinah* is not a physical or spiritual being, nor absent from *HaShem*.

the keys to kindness, caring for others, and nurturing those in need of affection.

What aspects must she work on?

She should make herself a whole vessel able to receive light from her husband, as I do from *Keter* and she must know how to distribute this light. It is very easy for her to use this sustenance mistakenly, on material things. Should she understand how to channel this light, not only does she receive more light on herself but also on the whole world, bringing to everyone peace and wholeness.

So, is a woman's task less than a man's since she is a vessel to receive?

As explained, a woman's task in life is no simple matter. Without her, her husband won't accomplish or succeed. She is his opposite in many ways and they bring out the best in each other. It isn't about equal rights, two entirely different beings, one that lives in water and one that lives on earth, should they be expected to perform the same? Apart, a man and a woman are lacking, it is only when these two come together that both become great and whole. So, it isn't a matter of which is more important. Should she be jealous of a man because he wears *tefillin*, and she wasn't given this *mitzvah*? Should the man be jealous that he can't experience childbirth? Together, both man and woman are a perfect vessel.

So, how does all this relate to the *Shechinah*?

My child, if you don't treat women with respect, how can you be expected to treat the *Shechinah* with any dignity? You have to have good midos and learn how to be selfless. Marriage and all relationships for that matter, teach a person how to live outside themselves. The *Shechinah* is attached to a person who isn't only thinking of themselves, like a woman, she is a giver and therefore, the *Shechinah* attaches to her easily. So, if a person is kind to his spouse, he will have the *Shechinah* more in his life.

THE MATERIAL WORLD

Shechinah, how does materialism effect our relationship with each other?

Just as an object takes up physical space, so too it occupies spiritual space. This especially holds true when you attach yourself to worldly matters. It decreases the room inside you that instead could be used to attach to G-dliness.

So, this being said, can I be attached to You through the material?

Certainly, if the material object is being used in order to perform a commandment or in order to come close to *HaShem*, then it is also elevated.

If this is the case, then I would assume that the more material matters a person owns, the more tools he has to elevate to *HaShem*.

This is usually not the case, as physical objects seem to have the power of confusing a person. Maybe at first a person assumes he will not become overly attached to worldly objects but, in the end, their power seems to grow.

I see what You mean; it can be a big challenge to attach the physical to the spiritual.

Generally, those owning fewer material objects seem to have greater spiritual abilities. Sometimes, though, people who are less attached to the material don't pay enough attention to physical cleanliness, and so they lack also cleanliness. It is not always a bad thing to be surrounded by material objects as long as one is not drawn in by them.

We should not underestimate the power materialism has to draw us in, leaving us attached more to the physical than the spiritual.

You must remember though my son how great it is when you utilize those things you already have for holy tasks. A single possession like a computer can be used for *parnasa*, *kiruv*, *chesed*, studying and to save one from wasting precious time. How ironic it is that the last thing I mentioned seems to be its greatest power of destruction.

Why does a tool that has so much capacity for good end up destroying so much?

Simply because you don't appreciate it enough and you are not thankful enough to *HaShem* for the positive things it can bring you. If you were, how could you ever come to sin through it? Material matter is like *Klipah Nogah*; it contains both good and bad and it's up to you to choose the good. At the same time though, you shouldn't use such an object unless you already have the strength to bring out its good. My child, realize your own strength for good!

CONNECTION TO SHABBOS

Shechinah, can you tell me about *Shabbos*?
    Shabbos is the light of the world; everything is sustained through the *Shabbos*. It is the center of the week; Sunday, Monday, and Tuesday draw from the light of the past *Shabbos*, and Wednesday, Thursday, and Friday from the coming *Shabbos*.

It's difficult to think of it as centered, as our calendars show Wednesday in the middle.
    Should you see it in the correct way, it is a life-altering experience. Not only should it be viewed as the center of the week, but also as the center of your life.

How are You connected to the *Shabbos*?
    Shabbos and I have something very much in common. Both our jobs are to bring the holiest light down to creation. The light of *Shabbos* lowers itself to such an extent that man can honor it by honoring his body. By feasting, donning nice clothing and other similar activities. I am connected to the *Shabbos* and the *Shabbos* also draws my light down to the people. There are so many *mitzvos* of *Shabbos* that bind a person to me. Should a person sanctify himself, the spiritual attainments that can be reached on the *Shabbos* are endless.

So where should I begin in my quest to attain the maximum amount of light from the *Shabbos*?

Separate yourself from weekday thoughts and activities: Dress differently, act, talk, think, eat and even study Torah differently.

Please continue to enlighten me.

How you go into the *Shabbos* and prepare for her parallels the light that will reflect back at you during the *Shabbos*. If while preparing for *Shabbos* you feel overwhelmed and frustrated, you are putting forth a form of light that will later reflect back on you. Only when you make provisions with love can you receive a light of love on *Shabbos*. Begin preparing on Wednesday; the light of *Shabbos* will shine for you and you will be happy; not only will I rest upon you completely, but so will the holy light of *Shabbos*.

CHANNELING ILLNESS

Shechinah, why do I suffer from illness?
    A person can be sick for many reasons. It could be to purify him from sin and it could also be to help him repent. The reason could also be that *HaShem* wants to draw a person close to Him; sickness gives a person reason to call out to Him.

If I am sick, are you close to me?
    When you are sick, *HaShem* sends Me to your bedside to comfort you. Just as He sent me to the home of Avraham after his *bris*, so too, He sends me to comfort everyone.

If my illness is because of sin, are You still there?
    HaShem sends Me to you but if you are impure, drawing further instead of closer to our Creator through your sickness, am I to stay? Sometimes people use illness as an excuse to fall into sin even further. Is this the way?

You are correct. We must be careful during illness to channel our actions in the right direction.
    Certainly by doing so, you will shorten the length of time you have to be in this condition. Also, when you return to health, your spiritual abilities and comprehension will have significantly multiplied.

I have learned from you an important lesson that illness can be of great benefit to me. Should I *chas v'shalom* be sick, I will be happy You are close to me and that

HaShem loves me enough to want me close to Him in holiness.

It is not just you that I am close with when you are ill. Anyone who visits the sick, I connect to them as well. That is why the _mitzvah_ of visiting the sick is so difficult for people. It is because it is so holy that the evil inclination makes excuses for them to avoid visiting the sick and doing this holy _mitzvah_. It is because if someone does visit the sick, it is such a holy task that it brings them forgiveness of sin.

I will try more to visit the ill.

If you do so, please be sensitive to the person you're visiting. Don't visit them in order to feel good about yourself but be there for the person to help them in all their needs. Comfort them and try to make their life easier. It isn't easy for a person to fall out of their regular pattern of life.

EMPTINESS

***Shechinah*, if you don't mind, can you explain to me why I feel emptiness inside after sinning?**
While sinning in body and mind, your soul has to undergo tremendous humiliation. What does a person do when humiliated? He tries to leave rather than suffer any more embarrassment. The greater parts of your soul do the same. I too leave, feeling the humiliation of a mother after her child commits a terrible deed.

Instead of suffering humiliation, why do you not choose to run away before my act of treason is completed?
I choose to stay as long as possible in hope that you would feel my pain and return to *HaShem*. Any mother would do the same for her child.

Shechinah, I did feel Your pain, but I felt I was too deep in my ways to just turn around, so I continued until I felt you leave entirely and then I was alone. The pain of separation from You is greater than any other pain in the world. How can I prevent this from happening again?
Remember Me often. Know that the evil one is a trickster telling you it's too late to turn back. It's never too late, my child. Don't follow his advice; cry out to *HaShem* to save you. When you are in pain, call Me as you would your mother. I will endure whatever humiliation I must just to hold you until your troubles pass.

I did call You, but you did not come to my aid.

In your heart, you had chosen the path of sin. You didn't call Me with an honest heart. I wanted to come. Know that I chose to be there for you with a full heart, if only you chose the same, and we would be inseparable.

CAN I REALLY KNOW YOU?

How difficult is it for me to bind myself to You?
    It's unfortunate that people underestimate their own ability and holiness, thinking, "I could never bind myself to the *Shechinah*."

I grew up learning to think in this way. When I spoke to others about the *Shechinah*, they just dismissed it; She was too high to comprehend, feel or take hold of.
    Doesn't a mother stop everything to embrace her children when they finally remember and appreciate her? Of course I am there and my presence is comprehendible. If only you wished to see me, I would come to your side more often. Shame on those who preach that the presence of the *Shechinah* isn't real and felt in one's heart. In fact, anyone who makes an effort to feel the holiness around them is commendable.

What else can I do in order to feel the *Shechinah* in my life?
    Every time you do a *mitzvah*, especially with joy, My presence is felt. Many people deny this feeling and push it off as unreal or just their own emotional pride instead of basking it its light. What I mean by this is that when you are blessed with My presence, you have the ability to create even more *mitzvos* and benefits. Without the holy presence of the *Shechinah*, one can still do *mitzvos* but with this holiness, one can accelerate their performance of the commandments. Therefore, it should be the goal of every Jew to connect to

Me and do their utmost to ensure My Presence doesn't leave them.

Can You define what it might mean to feel the *Shechinah* for some of us that aren't holy enough, never experienced, or don't know how to distinguish this true feeling verses one imagining something that is not a real feeling?

Well no two people think alike, look alike or feel things exactly the same. *HaShem* created everyone unique and to make their own personal connection to Him. To feel the presence of the *Shechinah*, is therefore subjective and individual but that truly is the beauty of it. To feel something that only you can experience. To then utilize this emotional feeling to feel connected to *HaShem* and do then perform even more service to Him. That is the purpose as to why *HaShem* created this idea of feeling the *Shechinah* and that the *Shechinah* would accompany the Jewish people in exile.

So, does this mean that when the exile is completed, and we have the new Temple, a person wouldn't need the presence of the *Shechinah* to be along with them?

HaShem created the Jewish people so that they can experience the light and beauty of *HaShem*. The *Shechinah* is this experience. It is the feeling one has in the Garden of Eden. It is the feeling *Klal Yisrael* has when the Temple is built, and it is something that can be experienced by those who perform *mitzvos lishmah*. The entire purpose of creation thereby is to feel the *Shechinah*. You have been blessed my children with so many ways to feel this holiness and there is no greater reward or connection in the world to make.

Tikkun Shechinah

DO YOU SURROUND ME

Shechinah, I have heard that being close to *tzaddikim* brings one closer to You. How is this so?

If you wanted to be close to someone of importance, you would secretly find out the names of those closest to him. Once getting to know them, you could travel alongside them to accomplish your true mission to be close to the man of importance. It is the same way with *tzaddikim*. The *tzaddik* worked hard over many years to come close to Me. If you befriend him he will take you with him as he climbs the spiritual heights, and I will descend upon you in his merit.

Wow, that is truly amazing; but why would the *tzaddik* want to do this for me?

It is one of his greatest pleasures to draw people close to *HaShem* and to bring the holiness of the *Shechinah* upon them.

Why does this make him so happy?

He understands that *HaShem's* true desire is to be close to His children; that man cannot live a true and happy life without the Divine Presence upon him, and that I in turn yearn to nurture My children and be with them in holiness.

So how do I begin this undertaking?

Find the chassidim closest to the *tzaddik* and draw close to them. They in turn will draw you close to the *tzaddik*. Once that happens, he can only fill your vessel with how much it can hold. Continue to work on self-discipline and purity and your vessel will become better able to hold more light from him.

At what point will You be with me?
When you are with the *tzaddik*, I will always be there. Do not lose hold of him in your heart and in the guidance he gives you. It is a great task to humble oneself to a teacher and leader. Ask yourself, how important is it to attach to the *Shechinah*? Will I continue to be afraid of drawing close to this *tzaddik* or will I devote my life to his guidance? Can this person draw me closer to *HaShem* than I am right now on my own? If so, wait no longer and reestablish your connection today!

YOUR PRESENCE UPON ME

Shechinah, why is Your Presence more apparent in a place where Jews gather to pray?

    HaShem has promised you this, that whenever ten men join to pray[22], He will send Me to you. Even if all ten are unworthy, nonetheless, I will be there yearning to unite with my love.

How do I feel Your Presence in such a situation?

    If you fear *HaShem* and your heart is clean and you are at peace with your fellow, you can feel my presence.

Happy are we, how good is our portion!

    Should you draw people closer to *HaShem*, you will feel My Presence all the more. This is because the greatest thing in life is helping others to be holy, pure and to increase their faith. When you draw people closer to Me, it therefore will uplift you to a much higher *madrega* of closeness.

---

[22] Berachos 6a

MY THOUGHTS

Shechinah, it gives me great pain to know that I have hurt You through my many sins.

I appreciate that you recognize My troubles but, rather than sit idly by and meditate on my sorrow, bind yourself to *HaShem* and lift Me up.

Aren't my thoughts of You lifting You up?

Yes, they are but, combined with a *mitzvah* for my sake, the good you can cause is beyond your comprehension.

Can you give me some examples?

While praying, You can meditate on lifting Me up. During studying, you can draw Me down to you. When you do a *mitzvah* with joy and *kavanah*, you lift the *mitzvah* up on high to a much further level.

How would I make a *kavanah*?

In the simplest way, a *kavavah* could be saying a blessing a little bit slower and paying more attention to the words your saying. When you do a kindness, it could be the idea of performing it without reward and for pure reasons like to elevate the world. On a higher level, one could pause slightly while saying *HaShem's* name and concentrate on holy combinations of letters. The main thing in *kavanah* is that one's intent should be completely pure and truthful.

MODESTY

***Shechinah*, in what way does modesty affect a person?**

Well, there are two aspects of modesty. One is how a person acts on the outside and the other is how modest the heart is. If a person is immodest on the outside, this in turn causes immodesty on the inside. Should a person pay close attention to his external modesty, chances are this modesty will eventually reach to his heart.

What are the laws of modesty ordained by our *rabbis*?

The laws differ for males and females. A male should be sure to wear a *kippah*, since it reminds him that he stands before a Higher Authority. *Chassidim* say the lower body should be covered by a long coat. While praying, he should cover his head with a hat and wear a jacket. *Chassidim* also suggest a *gartel* worn around the waist to separate the upper body from the lower body. Married women should cover their heads and all women their shoulders down past their elbows; the skirt below their knees, and the lower neck. There are many other laws.

What are some of the laws apart from clothing?

Not speaking to people of the opposite gender in the street is a form of modesty. This extends to inside a building as well; the talk should be shortened and take place only if there is a purpose to it. A man and a woman who are not close relatives should not put themselves in a position alone in closed quarters. These are some basic aspects; let us also not forget the importance of modest thoughts.

Once modesty reaches the heart, how does this benefit the soul?

The benefits are endless. A modest person is a HaShem-fearing person. When a person lives modestly and goes to pray, HaShem answers the prayers. I am also sent to be near the modest people and shine the light of holiness upon them. You cannot trick HaShem by pretending to be modest. HaShem knows all the thoughts of a person and the realness of his heart. Try to be real with yourself; let the modesty of your heart reflect a true external modestly. Expect nothing less from yourself and the chambers of your heart with glow with purity.

PART TWO

SHECHINAH, THE SECRET ELEVATION

The purpose of this *sefer* is to help you the reader feel a personal connection to the *Shechinah*. I hope that, after reading the first few chapters of Tikkun Shechinah, you are willing to do anything to bring her pleasure. When you care about the *Shechinah* with all your heart, it becomes impossible to spend your days idly.

It is important to find a completeness of self before attempting spiritual rectifications, or they might do more damage than good. *Chassidus* teaches that the purpose of a *rebbe* and *rabbi* is to bring the highest Torah secrets down to even a simple Jew. I am faced with a personal dilemma: Is it the proper time and place? Many of you have been wondering about these secrets for years and are quite capable of receiving them. Therefore, even though my knowledge in Kabbalah is brief, I will try to draw some of these beautiful secrets to you. The sages have told us that the more you study Kabbalah, the more you realize you lack understanding. I give you these secrets now to store away for the future, although for me personally they are avenues to great meditations. However, I advise against the actual practice until your soul is complete.

As you already know, there are ten holy Sefiros and holy worlds. With these Sefiros the entire world was created. In fact, these Sefiros are being recreated every moment of every day. They are extensions of HaShem's Divine will. Each of the four worlds: Asiyah, Beriyah, Yetzirah, Atzilus, has ten holy Sefiros.

Asiyah is generally referred to as the world we live in, where the sparks mostly fell during creation. It is this world that needs the greatest elevation and it is here that the *Shechinah* has its landing during the exile. *Yetzirah* is the world of the angels. *Beriyah* is the world of creation, providing the souls and the Throne of *HaShem*. In *Atzilus*, everything is brought into completion and extends directly from *HaShem's* light. There is no limitation here but complete *bitul* in *HaShem's* Oneness.

In order for something to work properly, there has to be a system. The worlds and *Sefiros* are the system of *HaShem's* internal Will. They do not create a separate entity besides Him. Everything that happens or that we see is all contained in His Divine Will. The *Shechinah* and *HaShem* are one entity and being. Thinking of these in duplicity is a huge mistake.

The highest *Sefirah* is *Keter*, Crown, which is from the concept of *AYN*, nothingness, because it is beyond our ability to comprehend. In fact, we are not allowed to think too deeply into this because it contains secrets of the creation of mankind. It is the realm of absolute mercy, bearing no sadness, no misery, no division; only glory, beauty and grace. This *Sefirah* is connected to the holy Name of *HaShem*. It is also represented by the crown of the *yud* in the Tetragrammaton, the name YKVK.

The next *Sefirah* is that of *Chachmah*, Wisdom. With *Chachmah*, He founded the earth. This is why it is also connected to that of *Ratzon*, *HaShem's* Will. It is here that the *Spheres* become perceivable. This is the place where one has access to request one's wishes. It is the origin where thought begins to flow. Even though it is not completely revealed, *Chachmah* isn't completely hidden. It is represented by the body of the letter *Yud* in YKVK.

Binah, our next *Sefirah*, is very important with regards to the *Shechinah*. It is represented by the letter *Hay* of YKVK.

A river went out from Eden… (Genesis 2:10) Going out from Eden, this is *Chochmah* that drew this benevolence from *Keter*. The river is *Binah*. "To water the Garden," that is to bring sustenance to *Malchus* and *Binah*. *Malchus* contains all the residue of blessing from the upper worlds as it comes down to us. *Binah* is considered the upper *Shechinah*, while *Malchus* is the lower *Shechinah*.

When we speak about the *Shechinah* in the lower realms, we are referring to the lower *Shechinah* in *Malchus*, Kingship. The elevation of sparks is this revelation of the lower *Shechinah* brought back up the ladder to *Binah*, which in turn connects *Binah* to *Chachmah* and *Keter*. *Malchus* is represented by the final letter *hay* of the Tetragrammaton.

In between these two is the letter *Vav*. The top half of the letter represents *Chesed*, *Gevurah*, and *Tiferes*; the lower part of the letter, *Netzach*, *Hod* and *Yesod*. Together, these Spheres connect *Binah* and *Malchus* and are a fundamental part of the *middos*, character traits through which *HaShem* reveals himself to us.

I would like you to close your eyes and imagine an hourglass with sand inside. When you flip it backwards, all the sand flows in the other direction. You turn it again and it returns in a backwards flow. This is similar to what the *Sefiros* are doing constantly. The light or, as you have imagined, sand, is constantly going up and down. All of the *Sefiros* are connected and one concept. It is just a matter of the flow, if it's free falling or has any obstructions that moment.

If you were now to think of a ladder, similar to that our father Yaakov had in his dream, each step is a different *Sefirah*. Angels and light flow up and down between the levels. If you were to take one of those steps away, the flow would be completely broken, but in our case, in this current exile, all the steps are there; the problem is just that they are broken. Much of the world's sustenance is caught in the flow between *Yesod* and *Malchus*.

Rebbe Nachman says, "If you believe you can break something, believe also there is a way to repair it. Now let us begin the lesson on repairing the broken vessels. To repair an item, the most important thing is to make sure the repairs are strong enough to hold the item together as if it were new. In the same aspect, the person repairing the *Shechinah* has to surround his soul with Torah commandments: Keeping *kosher*, observing *Shabbos* and so on. It is not just the observance but also the *Kavanah*, the thought process behind performing the action that is even more essential.

Even when not performing a commandment, one must embody fear and *emunah*, faith, in *HaShem*. One eye should focus on living life, and the other on his true mission in life. A person can actually stay connected to the *Shechinah* all the time. In fact, when we are doing the right thing, our souls naturally want to connect to Her. Only evil deeds and forgetfulness of *HaShem's* hand in our every action and breath seems to separate us. This is easily corrected through repentance and performing *mitzvos*.

The holy sages would meditate day and night on Torah thoughts. When faced with an unusual life experience, they would search for *HaShem's* mysterious ways within the event. When they found some explanation, the sages would connect it to *HaShem*, drawing the *Shechinah* into their lives.

Joy is also essential for dwelling with the Divine Presence. The sages have said in the Talmud: where there is sadness, the *Shechinah* leaves in a hurry. This is because sadness leads to sin and idleness. Maybe you can also assume that the *Shechinah* needs our happiness in order to feel comforted. Even though we should mourn for Her, we have to do so uprightly and with a clear conscience.

HaShem has many holy names through which He relates to creation. Each name of *HaShem* is holy and draws a person's thoughts to pureness. The names *EKYH, YKVK* and *Adna* are very important ones. Different combinations of these holy Names are able to repair many worlds. The worlds are affected even through different combinations of their *nekudos* and tones. There are twelve ways in which to envision

YKVK. This is parallel to the twelve *mazalos*, constellations, and the twelve tribes of Israel.

There are many ways to use combinations during your prayers and meditations. One can think of the Spheres in combinations of colors, in circles, spiritual hemispheric directions, ladders, black and white fire, red fire and more. There are hundreds of *Yichudim* which are known from the Arizal that are specifically designed to elevate the *Shechinah*. These techniques are available for the wise. Meditating on them is considered like Torah study; when a rabbi wasn't able to concentrate on a Torah passage or teaching, he would meditate on a simple or complex combination of holy letters.

"I saw a vision like fire, with a Glow (*nogah*) around it." (Ezekiel 1) The flashing fire in Ezekiel's vision alludes to the influx of prophecy that reached his mind. This is what *HaShem* told Jeremiah: "Are not my words like fire?" (Jeremiah 23:29) Jeremiah himself also said, "It was in my heart like burning fire." (Jeremiah 20:90)

Let us take the letters *YKVK*. The wise would see these letters in black fire on a white fire background. Smoke would rise from the letters as it did when Moshe Rabenu brought the tablets down from Har Sinai. The ability to see this meditation comes from a few points: The first is purity of body and soul. This comes from *mikvah* immersion and keeping far from impure thoughts. The second way is through regular meditation on this vision until it becomes more naturally apparent. Sometimes the ability is given as a gift after years of prayer and tears. Other times, it is handed down from one's *rabbi* and mentor. It is also something that shouldn't be forced. If the holy Name doesn't wish to appear before you in this way at this moment, it is important to be calm and wait.

The technique begins as follows: Start by creating a spiritual vision of the letter *Yud*. After you can see it, you might wish to enlarge it so that it fills your entire mind. It is easier to keep a thought if it is continuously moving, so you might wish to animate it or some object around it. Now take a match to it and light it on fire. The letter should start to flash a little. If it doesn't, maybe first start with a simple meditation, with a candle alone. Just as a child needs to practice crawling slowly and then to walk, so might you. If you are able, once the letter is on fire, you can start to feel its heat radiating your body. Fire is a hot substance and it is bright to one's eyes. If you do it correctly, you will even start to perspire and feel this imagination as something quite real. Now that the letter *Yud* should be flashing before you in red fire, you are now going to place the letter *Hey* next to this letter, letting both letters fill your entire mind. It will start flashing along with the *Yud*. Turn the flashing into an even brighter fire and let the two letters radiate your mind. Now bring in the third letter *Vav* and let it sparkle on fire. Relight all three letters with even more fire. Then bring inside the final letter *Hey*. Now all four letters are on fire and sparkling before you.

 My friends, this is only the beginning of our holy meditation. You can now turn this into a massive fire, glowing brighter, and envision the combinations of letters even larger in your mind. Start to see the smoke rising from the letter as it goes up to the heavens. Black smoke is going up out of the letters and white smoke surrounds them. All this smoke is rising up on high like that of the *karbonos*, sacrifices to *HaShem*. Keep this meditation with you and guard it from all impurities. This technique was taught to me personally by the Nikolsburg Rebbe *shlit"a*.

 Seeing the holy letters on fire and connecting to them was the way of the Baal Shem Tov's prayer. He explained how you should draw the letters out while saying them and yearn to keep them, all the while allowing them to float to heaven to form words, sentences and holy unity. This technique can be used during prayer, meditation and throughout the day, to remember *HaShem*. The *rebbe* also mentioned that while studying Torah, if you connect to the letters, you can find through them *ruach hakodesh*, Divine inspiration.

Glancing upon the holy Names in the form of color, as taught by Rabbi Moshe Cordevero, is also a great technique. The ladder of the *Sefiros* can be climbed through this. Looking at the name *YKVK* in white with the *nikud* of *segol* has the power to draw *Chesed* down from the heavens and reverse harsh decrees. If you think about a community, or a person in trouble, while meditating on this you can save many souls. There are many such techniques, and I am teaching you only a few in order to awaken your soul to serve *HaShem*.

The *Shechinah* is connected to *Malchus*, which is the letters *ADNA*. You can view this too with the techniques mentioned above. However, there is another way to consider: *ADNA* can be expanded using another technique in *kabbalah*. When you expand a letter, you get closer to its source. There is no end to expanding the letters and thus you can reach great levels of *bitul*, the feeling of nothingness, through them. Rabbi Chaim Vital experienced great pleasure when the Arizal would teach him something of letter expansions. *ADNA* is expanded by spelling out each letter in its full form. *ALEPH*- spelled *Aleph, Lamed,* final *Peh*. Then *DALED- Daled, Lamed, Daled*. Then the next letter *PEH* is spelled, *Peh* and then *Yud*. Continue on now to the letter *Daled* and so forth. Once finished, you can light these also on fire if you choose or you can further expand them as there is no end to this.

The reason why I have brought these meditative teachings is for you to understand the many ways *HaShem* gave His people for ending the exile and raising up the *Shechinah*: It can be through Torah study; the Talmud says, "Talmud Torah *keneged kulam.* (Torah study is equal to all the commandments)." You can also do it by increasing *kavanah* in *mitzvah* performance like prayer, *tefillin, brachos, Tikkun Chatzos, hachnasas orchim, bikur cholim,* honoring your parents and kind acts performed for another human being.

HaShem sent us into exile to elevate the hidden sparks but He didn't send us here alone. He gave us the *Shechinah* and Her holiness to keep us connected on High. Just as Her love for us is unconditional, so must ours be. Our holy mother Rochel wished to be buried along the road so those passing by could be comforted by her presence. Our holy matriarch gave everything she could to uphold Judaism for future generations. She is the embodiment of the *Shechinah;* it was her will to be connected to *HaShem* at all times. Just as it was her wish, so should it be ours.

If you want to connect to the Spheres, you can do so through meditation or by attaching yourself to the *middos*, character traits of *HaShem*. *Chesed* is the fourth Sphere. Its color is white and its main *nikud* is *segol*. *HaShem* is manifesting this *middah* to us when He shows outward kindness to us. As soon as you grasp that this is happening during your life, stop for a second and think about the source of *HaShem's middos*. By doing this, you elevate *Chesed* back up the chain; it climbs up to the Sphere of *Binah*. When you are walking by the road and see a white flower, think about how it draws its light from *Chesed*. Doing these things will connect you to the *Shechinah*.

Should you be in the midst of a thunderstorm, think of the Sphere of *Gevurah*, strength. Think of our holy father Yitzchok and how the judgment of *HaShem* is *Emes*. Meditate on fear of *HaShem* and elevate this storm and its *Gevurah* up through the chain till it reaches *Binah*. If you see a red rose, or simply the color red, you can imagine how it comes from *Gevurah* in this same way.

If you're visiting a beautiful mountain range, reflect on the Sphere of *Tiferes,* beauty. All beauty comes from *HaShem*; instead of ignoring it, you can elevate it in your mind up the ladder to *Binah,* maybe higher to *Chochmah* and even *Keter*. There are endless events that *HaShem* puts in front of you that can be elevated in thought or good deeds. Nothing that happens is ever a coincidence. Every item is a spark of the *Shechinah,* waiting to be uplifted by a *bracha,* a prayer or good deeds.

When you're faced with a sin and you refuse to give into the temptation, this too can elevate the *Shechinah*. The further something is from *HaShem*, the greater *tikkun* it needs and the more important it is to be elevated. This is why the greatest way to draw close to *HaShem* is to fix another Jewish soul and help him repent. When you do so, all his sins are elevated and moved to the scale of merit.

Even if you can't complete the task of drawing another person close to *HaShem*, by simply judging him favorably you can lift him up from judgment to merit and tip the scale for his benefit. This is the true secret of *Chassidus;* it is about elevating what surrounds you through an *ayin tov*.

Let's go through one last meditation to awaken our souls. If you take the name *YKVK*, the *gematria*, numerical value of the first two letters in expanded form is twenty-six. When we sin, we separate the last two letters of *HaShem's* Name, *Vav* and *Hey*. When we do *mitzvos* and elevate the *Shechinah*, the letters once again join the full name *YKVK* and it equals the *gematria* of twenty-six, with no need for expansion.

Now that your heart is warm for *HaShem*, you can take these concepts and develop them on your own. As people often say, knowledge is power. You now know many ways to rectify the *Shechinah*. Some are very simple while others are complicated and need more focus. The main thing is that your heart is sincere for *HaShem* and the Torah. Take upon yourself the responsibility to act uprightly and understand that our days in this world are short. There is much to accomplish and no time to waste. It is up to you; if not you, who will bring the final redemption? How many people are enlightened as you and aware of these important concepts? Just a very few.

PART THREE

TIKKUN CHATZOS AND CONNECTING TO THE SHECHINAH

When someone sets out to fix something, it is usually more of complicated job then the person first realizes. Generally speaking, if something breaks, it takes a person who has devoted some of his life to learning a craft and profession to mend it back together.

HaShem has given every Jew a special light with the ability to fix the world. Before our souls came into this physical world, we were taught the entire Torah and given a special ability to bring *tikkunim*. One of these is *Tikkun Chatzos*.

Tikkun Chatzos by definition means a remedy of the night. It carries the weight of ability to entirely fix Creation, the upper and lower worlds together. Repentance, joy, mourning, light, darkness and more are contained inside this *tikkun*. The entire world rests upon it, yet it bears some secrecy and hidden aspects which I would like to unveil.

When you ask someone slightly familiar with *Tikkun Chatzos,* he will first assume that it is a time when the great sages would arise from sleep in order to mourn the loss of the holy Temple. He might even tell you that this custom hasn't been practiced in hundreds of years and lacks importance. At the very least, he would have heard about the *tikkun* because of *Shavuos* night and the three weeks of restraint in which mourning for the holy Temple and night

Tikkun Shechinah

time Torah study are considered important. When you dig deeper though and become wise, you will find that the aspect of mourning is just one part of this rectification and that the *z'man* of *chatzos* is special in many more ways.

These aspects can't be understood just through wisdom; a person with a holy soul must understand them internally. There are a great many spiritual insights available during these special hours of the night. Each person on his own level will be able to leave with something holy.

> Excerpt from *sefer* Kavanos Halev:
> King David truly understood the importance of this hour as he constantly spoke of this often in the Psalms. "At midnight I will rise to give thanks to thee." (Psalms 119:62) He also said, "Awake my soul, awake lyre and harp, I will awaken the dawn." (Psalms 57:9) King Solomon also speaks of this practice and he stated, "Arise, cry out in the night at the beginning of the watches, pour out your heart like water in the presence of *HaShem*." (Lamentations 2:19) We are told, "If the Jewish people were more careful to arise for *Chatzos* their enemies would be subdued and would not impose any decrees against them." (Zohar Chai, Bereshis 77) Rebbe Nachman says, "This tikkun, rectification prayer, has the power of redemption. It sweetens harsh decrees." (Likutey Moharan 1:149)

Instead of focusing on the *Tikkun* prayer itself, which you can read in my *sefer* Kavanos Halev or later on in this book, I would like to focus on the holy hour of *Chatzos* and its connection to the *Shechinah*.

> Excerpt from *Sefer* Kavanos Halev:
> The night is divided into many watches. During the first part of the evening, the world undergoes its daily judgment and the *kelipos* have access to higher levels, drawing greater nourishment. If this were to be unchecked, the forces of the other side would have too much power and this would adversely affect creation a great deal. However, the *kelipos* become ensnared by the *mitzvos* and Torah study that we

perform down below and the *kelipos* lose power. This happens at *chatzos*, when the first traces of *Chesed's* light start to manifest in the world. The rectification of *Malchus* then begins, when judgments are stayed and loving-kindness begins to be revealed. (Zohar 1:92b) Dovid Hamelech once recited, "I will rise up at midnight to give thanks to You for your righteous judgments." (Psalms 119:62)

The study of Torah after *chatzos* diminishes the forces of evil. (Zohar 1,248) The forces of un-holiness are overcome, and a person's sins are forgiven. One's intellect and thoughts become purified and one can grasp *HaShem's* unity without confusion. Everyone who wants to come closer to *HaShem* should drive slumber from his eyes at night, devote himself to Torah study, and pray in order to triumph over the "husks." This will positively help him come nearer to HaShem. (Reishis Chockmah, Sha'ar HaKedushah 7)

All hours of the day are important and have great significance in the worlds above. Since the entire world is sustained from the heavenly realms, we too are affected by the changing of the watches. Just as things in this lower world are constantly moving around, so too this happens up above. Instead of people, it is angels, holy lights and departed souls that are moving. Some have attained the greatest rewards in the Garden of Eden, while others are repairing their souls in *Gehenom*

There is a debate in the Talmud as to how many watches there are in each day, but the two we are focusing on here are the watches at midnight and that of the morning. At the beginning of each watch, some angels retire, and others are created or renewed in their place. The job of this group of angels is to sing praises to *HaShem* in simple purity.

Our *rabbis* remind us how great it is to say praises to *HaShem*. It was taught in the academy of Rabbi Yishmael: Even if Israel merited no other privilege than to greet their Father in Heaven once a month, it would be sufficient for them." (*Kiddush Levanah*, the blessing of the new month)

Greeting *HaShem* and praising Him is just one part of our *avodah*, but it is underestimated at times. We can learn from the angels how significant a chant of praise truly is when we comprehend that a simple angel can be created even just once in order to utter praises to *HaShem*. *Chazal* teach us that our souls are significantly greater than those of the angels. Should we recognize the power of praise and heartfully sing to *HaShem*, what more could He want from us, especially at the midnight hour.

An angel doesn't have free-will to pick and choose how it will perform for *HaShem*. We on the other hand can reach the greatest levels of *tikkun* when we desire to serve *HaShem lishmah*, with all our hearts. The Shelah says, "A man who arises regularly for *tikkun chatzos* is a *tzaddik*. He is considered a member of the Court of the King and his *parnasa* is assured." (Prayer book of the Shelah)

What the Shelah means by saying he is a member of the Court is that he is connected to the *Shechinah*. We learn from the Zohar that the *Shechinah* cries out at this hour, more than at any other hour, wanting to be united with Her children., Those wanting to be close to their Mother cannot ignore these cries, and therefore they too wake up to comfort Her. Why has She fallen from such great heights? It is because our many sins have separated Her and caused Her to come down to the lowest levels of *Asiyah* to help Her children survive this exile. Would a mother ever abandon her children to suffer alone? Of course, *HaShem* too cries over the separation of the *Shechinah* and His holy Abode, which is empty.

The *Shechinah* has been told at this hour, "Go and reduce yourself," and is lowered to the worlds of *Briyah*, *Yesirah* and *Asiyah* (Creation, Formation and Action). These spheres are beneath her dignity; the honor due to the King's daughter really belongs in the *Sefirah* of *Atzilus*. This causes Her tremendous pain and she wails and screams to be united with *Keter* once again. King David, who was attached to Her in the root of *Malchus*, felt this pain more than the common man and he created the prayers of *Tikkun Chatzos,* which is our way of crying out along with Her. One's mother is always comforted with words of consolation from Her children.

As long as we are in exile, so too the *Shechinah* is here along with us to help us bear this long exile. The gematria of *Shechinah* is the same as that of *yeshua. The Shechinah* needs a new salvation every day, which depends upon *Bnei Yisrael* through prayers, good deeds and Torah study. (Alef Binah 28)

Anyone who does not share the pain of the *Shechinah* and the destruction of the Temple will not merit seeing its redemption and joy. As it says, "Celebrate a great rejoicing with her, all those who mourn over her." (Yeshiyah 66:10) Most people interpret this verse in future tense, but I believe it is also true in the present tense. This is because when a person takes upon himself to worry for the *Shechinah*, he becomes completely bound to Her. If you're connecting to such a holy light then you are fastening to all the great aspects your soul needs, to be in tune with *HaShem*. Fear of *HaShem* will be implanted within your very being. Faith will come easily.

By doing all that is possible to bring about the unity of the worlds, you are part of the redemption itself. You are bringing gladness to *HaShem* and the *Shechinah*, and this unity is the greatest joy. Each week on *Shabbos* or *Yom Tov*, the *Shechinah* is completely united with *HaShem* in *Atzilus*. A wise person can feel this joy within his observance of the holy day. So too can a person feel the great salvation when he brings about this daily unity. One of my greatest joys is when I have studied Torah through the night and then bound this study to the morning prayer at sunrise; it's like standing on top of the world after accomplishing something great.

Just as a person must be zealous to arise at night for Torah study, so must he be doubly and triply careful to rise early in the morning for prayers at the synagogue, since both provide a rectification of the *Shechinah*; from midnight onward the rectification begins, but only at the morning service is it completed. Therefore, one should rise with alacrity to pray at daybreak, as is proper, and be careful to come early to the synagogue, for this completes the *Shechinah's* rectification which begins with the prayer at midnight. (Petuchei Chotem-*Vayeitzei*)

This is similar to the *chupah*, which the wise know is the unity of the *Shechinah*, the bride, and *HaShem*, representing the groom. The bride and groom begin by walking towards the *chupah*. She walks around seven times, representing the seven *Sefiros* the *Shechinah* must climb in order to be rectified and united. As she circles, so does She become elevated, purifying those elements that attached to Her. Darkness is turning into light. Every time the *Shechinah* is elevated, we are one step closer to the final redemption.

The Baal Shem Tov taught, "Be sure to do the Midnight Service [continue through dawn] and bind together day and night [in Divine service] (Tzavaas HaRivash, p.12). Rabbi Tzvi Hirsh of Ziditchov said, "Many of our early forbears who had the Holy Spirit told us to bind together day and night through Torah and prayer. (Yifrach biYamav Tzaddik, p. 39b)

Rabbi Elijah deVidas has some encouraging words to help a person break the inner barriers that might stop a person from performing the nighttime rituals. He says, "Your yetzer will argue that you should not get up lest you harm yourself and your health. [But he says that you should resolve to get up] even if you see that you get a headache from doing so. Do not let that stop you from keeping up the practice the next day and [so] on. So, keep on day after day, and help will come to you from heaven, for the Torah says that "He who keeps a mitzvah will come to no harm," and "That which is good will not be withheld from he who acts in sincerity"; for the Torah is only won through intense self-sacrifice. [And he says:] Before you go to sleep, or during the blessing "He who hears prayer" in the Shemoneh Esreh, you should pray that the Holy One, blessed be He, help you to get up at midnight and to stay awake until daytime. (Totzaos Chaim, p. 22, 23, 25)

I have found that when a person really wants to do something, he is able to banish much physical regularity in order to do something he enjoys. In these instances, a person might not have the *Shechinah* with him, yet he is able to continue on even with little sleep. As the *tzaddik* mentioned here, at first a person could feel fatigue but, once the energy of the *mitzvah* takes over, the physical doesn't seem to be so important.

Staying awake until the morning light isn't necessary but is highly beneficial, as the sages mentioned. Even the great *rabbis* who woke themselves to perform the *tikkun* found the pull towards relaxing the body too strong and would tire soon after. There is no shame in this but if you have made it to the ninetieth yard, you still haven't scored a touchdown. It was a great run and a miraculous ego boost for the team. In fact, you have strengthened your spiritual capabilities and lifted up the *Shechinah* to new heights but if you would just go a little bit more, you will score points that secure a great win for *Klal Yisrael*. The Baal Shem Tov once stated, "Prayer at sunrise is like the difference between east and west." This statement speaks for itself.

Let us go into more detail to better understand this unity between night and day. The *rabbis* said: The song of Torah is only [heard] at night, as it says: "Arise, sing out at night." (Eicha [Lamentations] 2:19) Whoever involves himself with Torah at night will have a strand of kindness extended over him during the day, as it says: "During the day, G-d ordains his kindness, and at night, His song is with me, a prayer to the living G-d". (Tehillim 42:9)

Even though it is a *mitzvah* to study during the day and at night, it is only at night that a person gains most of his wisdom. Therefore, anyone who wishes to earn the "Keter Torah", should be careful with all of his nights, not to waste even one of them sleeping, eating, drinking, talking (idly) etc., but rather studying Torah and words of wisdom. (Rambam Talmud Torah: 13)

The Medrash reports that when Moshe *Rabeinu* ascended Mt. Sinai, he was able to differentiate between night and day: HaShem would teach him the written Torah (the twenty-four books of Tanach) during the day, and at nighttime the Oral Torah. (Mishna, Talmud etc.)

Based on this, the *mekubalim* say that one should refrain from studying *Mikrah* at night. The Mishna Berura explains that at most it is a matter of preference, not forbidden. The *Yesod V'Shoresh HaAvodah* and other Kabalistic works write more strongly against studying Torah *shebechesav* at night.

The Gemara in Eruvin (65b) says that night was created solely for Torah study. I think it was repeated in the name of Rav Aharon Kotler that what one does during the day is what he is obligated to do: Work, take care of his family and community. Nighttime is synonymous with rest and relaxation and doing what we choose to do. It is when we naturally revert to our default positions.

If someone is so involved and enthralled with learning Torah to the point that his default position is to sit down and study Torah, then *HaShem* says I will give you a special *bracha* in that Torah learning: The ability to acquire the most wisdom during that session; and you will have a special *chein*, throughout the day.

As explained before, at the beginning of the watches in heaven there is much movement in the heavenly realms. The angels are going up and down, right and left as they change places. Souls are going up and down the Chariots. New *shiurim*, are forming and new praises are being said. There is a huge difference between greeting these new sessions on time and joining them late. Those who arrive early find greater benefits than those arriving late. There is a certain *kavod*, by eagerly joining in the changes of the watches. Your prayers can ascend with greater certainty and precision.

Many *tzaddikim* are careful to start the new day with sunrise, and the evening with *mincha* prayer just before *shekiya*. This is followed by Torah study in between nightfall and complete darkness; then to say *maariv* prayers just after *Rabbenu Tam zeman*, before other activities. After a brief nap, they awaken for midnight to show *HaShem* their true devotion. These are the ways of those who have spiritual strength.

For us, just learning about these spiritual pathways opens doors for us in wisdom and understanding. It may not be practical for us to practice these *hanhagos*, regularly, due to our family responsibilities. However, even the little we do grants us new revelations and inner resolutions.

Many of our struggles in life can be solved, though, through the nighttime and early morning rituals. The sages have said that at night, since the song of *HaShem* is with us, it is an easier time to do *hisbodidus*, and speak to *HaShem*. Repentance becomes more heartfelt and our sins are easily forgiven.

Rabbi Tzvi Hirsh complements these actions and says, "But know this too, my brothers, that I have received a tradition from our *rabbis* that *Tikkun Chatzos* arouses on High a special time of Divine favor, when a man's misdeeds will be forgiven. My brothers, there is no better time for *hisbodidus* and for separation from the worldly things, when worldly thought will not disturb you, than at midnight. That is the time to arouse yourself to stand up and pray for the welfare of your despondent soul, which through her sins has been removed from the source of pure living waters and coarsened through involvement with the body, which has its root in the lowly dust.

"At this hour you should each do well to uncover those things you have done that are worthy of shame, and you should speak from your heart to *HaShem*, like a servant before his master, with bowing and prostrating, lying on the ground and crying out verses about *HaShem's* mercy; to speak like a son before his Father. All that he says in prayer should be in his native tongue that he speaks and understands, so that he can pour out his soul without hindrance and can express fully the pain of his heart over his sins and transgressions. He should beg pardon and forgiveness. You should beg *HaShem* who made you and formed you and created you, to come to your aid and bring you close to His service, so you will revere Him with all your heart."

This teshuvah is the whole purpose of arising at midnight. When you consider all this before sleep, pray that from Heaven they will wake you at midnight [that you will succeed in getting up then], and then you will go to sleep without worries and be at peace. (DhTvh Y, Hashkamas ha-Boker, #22)

Rabbi Elijah deVidas said, "It seems to me that this practice is a basic pillar for all service of HaShem. It is also not by accident that the service at midnight is emphasized so much throughout the Zohar, innumerable times, more so than all the other *mitzvos*." (Totzaos Chayim p.23) Rebbe Nachman once remarked, "A Jew's main devotion is to rise at midnight." (Sichos Haran, #301)

In the words of the Komarno Rebbe, to rise at midnight to study, sing and pray to G-d is, "A taste of the World to Come," something whose spiritual value is actually felt and experienced. May we merit connecting to this light of the Divine Presence!

PART FOUR

STORIES ABOUT THOSE WHO AROSE DURING THE NIGHT

Rebbe Nachman teaches that stories have the power to wake a person up from a deep spiritual slumber. It is for this reason that I chose to share with you some beautiful stories of those who made sure to connect themselves with the *Shechinah* at all times. Some of these ideals you might find beyond your capabilities yet, but, through reading about them, a spark of righteousness will surely enter your heart.

Rabbi Velvel Cheshin once spoke of a certain *kabbalist* who used to study with his students at midnight. They once noticed that, outside the window, hosts and throngs of people were gathered around, as if listening to a concert. He explained to his students that every night the souls of the *tzaddikim* come to listen to their learning, but this one time they merited to actually see this; for *chatzos* is a portal to the next world.

Reb Levi Yitzchok Bender's personal study schedule was legendary. He gave himself over to following Rebbe Nachman's teaching, to finish many of the holy writings each year. His meticulousness in following the *rebbe's* advice to recite *Chatzos* and practice *hisbodedus* was also astounding. For some seventy-five years, he never missed a night of *chatzos*. Someone asked him, "Which of your accomplishments is most precious to you? Which are you going to present to the Heavenly Court?"

Reb Levi Yitzchok answered simply and in true *Breslav* fashion: "I lived thirty years in Russia and I still believe in G-d!" He was quite humble about the entire ordeal.

The Baal Shem Tov, of blessed memory, was very particular about praying at dawn. At times, when he did not have a *minyan* with which to pray [before dawn], he would pray alone. (Tzava'as HaRivash 16)

Some sages felt so strongly about this practice that they couldn't imagine another *rabbi* not observing it. Reb Shimshon from Ostropol saw in a dream that his place in *Gan Eden* was next to Hershel from Krakow, who was then a prominent *Rosh Yeshiva*, a *rav* in Lublin, and the head *dayan* in Krakow. Reb Shimshon began to worry about it. "I will be next to this *rav*? What will be with me? Maybe this *rav* is submerged in the desires of this world, running after money - rich - with a beautiful house. If this is the case, maybe it's really a punishment! Maybe I need to pray to cancel this decree?" He decided to travel to the *rav* and see for himself. Reb Shimshon dressed up like a poor beggar, knocked on his door and inquired, "Would it be all right for me to stay here a few days?"

What was Reb Shimshon doing there? What was he looking for? What did he want to check? He wanted to see if the Rav from Lublin cried at *chatzos*. One night he heard a sound from one of the rooms; he drew closer and heard heartfelt cries. He opened the door and found the *rav* of Lublin in a sea of tears, sitting on the ground and crying over the *churban*. Reb Shimon said, "*Baruch* HaShem, now I know that I will be able to rest in peace."

The Ribnitzer Rebbe was considered a great Chassidic miracle worker. He lived in the USSR under Josef Stalins rule, yet lived a fully religious Jewish life. He served as a *mohel* and a *shochet*.

He fasted often and immersed himself many times daily in water that was sometimes accessible only by chopping away at thick ice. His *tikkun chatzos* was observed while wrapped in sackcloth and ashes. Regularly it lasted six to seven hours, sometimes as long as twelve. He cried so much during *tikkun chatzos* that, when he was done, the tears and ashes mingled, and he was sitting in mud. The Russian gentiles feared and revered him. Officers of the KGB brought their wives and children for blessings, having experienced many miracles.

Reb Nochum Chernobler was once at an inn and he arose at midnight to say *tikkun chatzos*. The innkeeper, a very simple Jew, heard Reb Nochum reciting Psalms in the middle of the night. Confused, he went down and asked him, "What are you saying?"

Reb Nochum explained, "I am saying *tikkun chatzos* that the Master of the world should end our bitter *galus,* that we should all go to *Eretz Yisroel,* and it should be finally over."

The innkeeper was impressed. He went back upstairs, woke up his wife and told her, "You know, there is a Jew downstairs who is praying that the *galus* should end and that we should all go to *Eretz Yisrael.*"

His wife turned over and said, "Go to *Eretz Yisrael?* What is going to be with the farm? What is going to be with the cows? What is going to be with the horses?"

The innkeeper was bothered by his wife's questions. He went back to Reb Nochum and said, "But Reb Nachum - what will be with the farm, the cows and the horses?"

Reb Nachum responded, "You're worried about the cows, the house and the barn? So, when the Cossacks come, the Tartars come, and they pillage and plunder - then you're happy? Is that what you want? G-d will take us to *Eretz Yisrael.* There will be no more Cossacks and no more Tartars!"

Again, the innkeeper was impressed. He ran back upstairs and related Reb Nachum's response to his wife. The wife replied, "Go tell Reb Nachum that G-d should take all the Cossacks and all the Tartars to *Eretz Yisroel*. We'll stay here with the farm and the cows and the horses!"

This is what it means: One is *sovel* the *galus*. If one doesn't leave the '*sivlos*' of Egypt - if one can still tolerate it - then redemption is still far away.

Upon the completion of the holy *Shabbos*, when Reb Baruch [the landowner] lay down to go to sleep, he unexpectedly saw a light through his window. He got up from the bed and went to the window to see where the light was coming from; from one of the rooms of his neighbor's house. Reb Baruch was surprised at this and became very afraid, for he thought, maybe *chas v'shalom* a fire had broken out. So, he hastily dressed and ran to see what this light came from. As he approached the door of the room and looked through the keyhole, he saw the poor man [the Baal Shem Tov] sitting on the ground. The rabbi was saying, with great trembling, *tikkun chatzos*. He was up to the verse, "Why have You forgotten us for so long; why have You left us abandoned for such length of days?" While his hands were spread and raised, his face was shining brightly with a great light, and tears were running down his cheeks. (Sippurei Chasidim, ZEvin, vol. 1, #268)

Reb Shmelke, the head of the religious court of Nikolsburg, was once studying Torah with his holy brother Rabbi Pinchas. Both of them had already remained awake together for a number of nights with no sleeping, studying while standing on their feet the entire time. Rabbi Pinchas could not find the strength to continue; he got himself a pillow to lean on, so he could finally take a little nap. His elder brother Reb Shmelke reproached him, saying, "Brother! How can you stop from learning the holy Torah, parting from that which is of everlasting worth, for a transient pleasure?"

His brother Reb Pinchas responded, "Don't you see that I haven't the slightest bit of strength left with which to continue?"

Reb Shmelke explained, "But I was speaking to you just about this moment that you used your energy to walk over and get a pillow for yourself. You could have applied that energy differently and remained standing and learning." (Mekor Chayim, p. 100, #333) (Sefer Kavanos Halev Torah)

One scholar of that same generation, Rav Meir Karinsnofler, *av beis din* of Brodt and author of Yad haMeir, once wrote of his attempts as a youth to enter Reb Shmelke's yeshiva. He traveled to Reitshval, where Reb Shmelke cautioned him, "The main condition for studying here is that you never willingly go to sleep during the week." Rav Meir agreed, and for two full days he sat and studied consistently. By the third day, he could hardly keep his eyes open. Reb Shmelke began to deliver a complex lesson in the Gemara. Suddenly he required a certain book from his private study and sent Rav Meir to get it. As Rav Meir wearily combed through the bookshelf, he noticed the *rebbe*'s bed right beside it. Sleep overpowered him. He grabbed a pillow and dropped to the floor.

After a while, Reb Shmelke directed another student to look for the book and for Meir. The student returned and reported that Meir was sleeping on the floor.

"Does he have a pillow?" Reb Shmelke inquired. "Yes," the student replied.

"Too bad; because, if he didn't have a pillow, I would let him sleep; he had no other choice. But, since he had the time to put a pillow under his head and he went to sleep willingly, go wake him up."

Rav Meir, having awoken, realized what happened. He asked Reb Shmelke for his blessing and returned home.

When Rabbi Tzvi Hirsh of Ziditchov was in Lublin, he visited the court of his master the Seer of Lublin. Rabbi

Yaakov of Radzimin was also visiting their rabbi. Before dawn the Seer asked Rabbi Tzvi Hirsh, "Rabbi Hirsheli, has morning come?"

"The daylight has certainly arrived," answered Rabbi Tzvi.

The Seer then told Rabbi Yaakov to go outdoors and take a look at the sky. He went out and saw that it was still dark; but, since they realized that the Seer wanted it, they agreed with him and returned saying that it had already become day. The Seer then remarked: "It is still dark, but through the *tikkun chatzos* that we did we have clarified the darkness into day." (Ha-Hozeh mi-Lublin, p.138)

Reb Dov of Tcherin very much wanted to wake up at midnight to recite the *chatzos* prayer but found it impossible to rise. When nothing else worked, he hired a man to wake him and stand over him until he got dressed. Unfortunately, because he wasn't getting sufficient sleep, Reb Dov began suffering terrible migraines. Finally, Rebbe Nachman told him that his personal *chatzos* was three in the morning, thus providing him a few more hours of unbroken sleep. "Sleep and eat, just watch your time," the *rebbe* said to him. After this, those *chassidim* who awoke during the wee hours of the morning knew exactly when it was three a.m., for Reb Dov's arrival at the synagogue would give it away. (Kokhavey Or, p. 25 #21)

When word reached Reitshval about Reb Dov Baer, the great Maggid of Mezritch, Reb Shmelke and his brother, the Hafla'ah, decided to pay him a visit. "Why do *tzaddikim* like you have to travel so far to see me?" The Maggid inquired of them on their first meeting. When they remained silent, he continued, "So I will tell you. A person can arise at midnight to pray and learn until dawn with great concentration. Later he can recite the morning prayers with such holiness that he ascends through all the supernal worlds. However, if after his prayers he feels the slightest bit of pride,

Heaven takes all of his prayers and Torah, crumbles them up into a ball and throws them into the abyss!"

The two brothers, motivated to their very depths, replied, "The *rebbe* is right; we did not need to travel to meet him. We needed to crawl to him on our hands and knees!"

"What did you learn in Mezritch?" friends asked Reb Shmelke upon his return to Reitshval.

"Before I met the Maggid," he said," I fasted so my body could bear my soul. In Mezritch, I learned how the soul can bear the body!"

It was Reb Dovid of Lelov's way to hide his true greatness in Torah. No one ever saw him studying. He would hide in the attic to remain undisturbed. In the depths of winter, he would wrap his feet with pillows and continue studying; but whenever he heard someone coming up the stairs, he would hurriedly hide his book away.

Once, Reb Dovid's brother-in-law, Rabbi Chaim Beldechovitz, decided to visit him, and Reb Dovid prepared a bed for him in the attic. Reb Chaim, anxious to grab a glimpse of his brother-in-law studying, only pretended to fall asleep. Later that night, Reb Dovid came up to the attic and opened a Tikkunei Zohar. Abruptly he arose and approached the bed. "Chaim, aren't you asleep already?" A deep slumber fell over the young man, and he saw nothing of Reb Dovid's nighttime activities. So precious were these to him that he wanted to keep it a secret.

It is said of Rebbi Zusya of Hanipol that it was his holy way that after praying the Evening Service he would learn Torah through the whole night standing up, and he slept only but two hours. (Mazkeret Shem ha-Gedolim, p.64)

When Rabbi Elimelech of Lizensk went into a personal "exile" to share the suffering and exile of the *Shechinah*, he once visited Pshevorsk, arriving there after midnight. Seeing that light was coming from a nearby window, he went there to look around. That was the home of the holy *rabbi*, Rabbi Moshe of Pshevorsk, the memory of a holy *tzaddik* for a blessing, and Rabbi Elimelech asked if he would allow him to lodge there for the night. Rabbi Moshe replied, "I just now got up [this was to perform the midnight vigil], so you are welcome to lie down in my bed."

When Rabbi Moshe thought that his guest was fast asleep, he began to recite the Psalms softly; but when Rabbi Elimelech heard him, he got up from the bed and stood beside Rabbi Moshe. When Rabbi Moshe noticed him, he motioned him to return to sleep; and he lay down once again. But when Rabbi Moshe started to say Psalms yet again, Rabbi Elimelech jumped up and stood next to the table at which Rabbi Moshe was sitting. Once more he motioned him to go to sleep [he did not want to interrupt his recitation with profane speech].

This transpired still a third time, until finally Rabbi Moshe rebuked him for disrupting his recitation. "How can I sleep" retorted Rabbi Elimelech, "when I see King David standing next to you!" Hearing this, and realizing this was no ordinary person, Rabbi Moshe said to him, "Are you Melech?" [Although he did not know him, Rabbi Elimelech's reputation had reached Pshevorsk]. And they excitedly began to make each other's acquaintance. (Sifran Shel Tzaddikim, p. 19, #3)

Rabbi Eliahu di Vidas inscribes in his Reshis Chochmah, "I heard that the sage, Rabbi Josef Tiatatzak, of blessed memory, did not sleep in a bed for forty consecutive years, excluding Shabbos. It is told that he used to sleep on a box, with his feet hanging down, and that he would arise at midnight. Nobody knew of his practices, and it was only revealed by his wife after he left this world. (Reshis Chochmah, Kedusha 7,154c)

With the help of *HaShem*, one day may you too be among the righteous who have stories told about them for future generations. The time of *chatzos* is one of humility and pureness. It leads you to a very special connection to the *Shechinah* and *Klal Yisrael*. You will most likely be so excited about the practice that you will want to share it with others, but only the devout will understand you and join you. As a reward for connecting to the *Shechinah*, you will find your sustenance taken care of from *HaShem* and increased blessing in all the things where you place your efforts.

PART FIVE

INTRODUCTION TO TIKKUN ROCHEL AND LEAH

As you know from the Chumash, two holy Matriarchs were the mothers of the tribes of Israel, Rochel and Leah. In the merit of their selflessness, they represent the two aspects of rectifying and rising up the *Shechinah*. We name the two prayers said at *chatzos* after them both.

It is written in Jeremiah (31:14), "Thus said *HaShem*: A voice is heard on high, wailing, bitter weeping, Rachel weeps for her children; she refuses to be consoled for her children, for they are gone."

I don't believe you have anyone in Jewish history who felt so strongly about the pains of exile. Therefore, it is only right to name the first *tikkun* after Rachel.

Tikkun Rachel encompasses in its text the heartfelt prayers of *Dovid HaMelech*, *Yirmiyahu* (Jeremiah) and other Sages. It starts with prayers of confession to HaShem and then moves on to some very moving Psalms. There are words of hope, but most are words of sorrow or lamentation in order to arouse your heart to repentance.

"Leah had beautiful eyes" (Genesis 29:17). She was able to perceive HaShem's hand in all things. Therefore, it is right that the next prayer belongs to her and so it is called *Tikkun* Leah. It Includes, prayers for salvation, comfort, praise and hope. This was Leah's way in life, always to find the good in each situation and remain hopeful. Her prayers are filled with many Psalms of Dovid and finishes by reciting the procedures the *kohanim* would perform in the *Bais Hamikdash*.

Dovid HaMelech had a great understanding of the source of prayer. He gathered these prayers and made a forth *zeman* of prayer service for the exceptionally righteous. He called it *Tikkun Chatzos* and devoted his life to comforting the *Shechinah*.

Rabbi Hiya opened his discourse with the verse: "Rejoice with Jerusalem, and be glad with her, all you that love her, rejoice for joy with her." (Isaiah 66:10) Come and see: When the Temple was destroyed and the Children of Israel were exiled from their land because of their sins, G-d's (Presence) departed (from) above. Wherever Israel was exiled the *Shechinah* followed them also into exile.

When He descended, He saw that His house was burnt. He looked at His people and behold, they were in exile. He asked for the Matron [the *Shechinah*] and learned that she was exiled. Then, it is written, "And on that day did G-d, the L-rd of Hosts call to weeping, and to mourning, and to baldness, and to girding with sackcloth." (Isaiah 22:12) And regarding her [the Shechinah] - also Her - what is written about Her?

"[The *Shechinah*] laments like a virgin, girded with sackcloth for the husband of her youth [Zeir Anpin]…" (Joel 1:8) Because "…he is gone, for He has left her, and they are separated." (Zohar Vayigash 210b)

Never did King David miss awakening at this important time for study and prayer. He understood that it was a responsibility for every righteous person. Rochel Imainu was to him like his own mother; the *Shechinah* was really like his sister; elevating the fallen sparks that continue our long exile was something real to him. To be devout in the commandments which elevate the evils of the world, it is the only way to bring the final redemption.

Besides these two prayers at midnight, midnight risers own up to their sins and learn Torah in a singular way.

I always felt a need to personify the first few minutes of *chatzos*. I would sing songs, shout praises and dance a little before reciting the *tikkun*. I had to transcend the blues to connect to *HaShem* and the Garden of Eden.

The world has always felt too sad for me; I let loose and grow warm at this hour of heavenly light, trying to make a positive spin on the idea of mourning and refection. I am pondering thoughts of hope and excitement for the future instead of only dwelling on the past.

In the initial blowout, as the new watch takes over and infinite favor gradually shines forth, I see the first watch of the night, din judgment; at this moment a pinhole of compassion radiates and slowly expands through the night. I finish this at sunrise prayers, after a night full of Torah study and supplications.

Everyone who mourns over Yerushalayim merits to see her joy (Taanis 30b). It is a fact that all a person's faculties are drawn after his thoughts. Wherever his thoughts go, that is where his very essence is drawn. So, when a person draws holy thoughts and yearns over

Yerushalayim, his thoughts and spirit are bound up with holiness. The expression, "he merits" (*zoche*), connotes purification. By weeping over Yerushalayim one is purified. Then, even today, one can experience a scent of the joy of Yerushalayim as it will be in time to come (Kedushas Levi).

At this hour, connecting to the *Shechinah* can plug you into the joyful times of the future. Those who haven't experienced it think of *chatzos* as an hour of mourning and darkness. It is just the opposite, though.

Shlomo HaMelech says, "I love the ones who love Me, and the ones who desire Me, will find Me." (Proverbs 8:17) If you found out the secret time and place where a benevolent king planned to be, wouldn't you go there? Wouldn't you look for him? The herald calls out and says, "*Uri tzafon, uvoy teman* (wake up winds of the North and come winds of the South), refresh my garden to distill its fragrances, and come my loved one to my garden and eat its delicious fruits." (Song of Songs 4:16)

Rebbe Shimon Bar Yochai taught: At that moment of *chatzos*, HaShem joins the *tzaddikm* in the Garden of Eden and they all listen below to those who study the Torah at this precious hour. So, my holy friends, do you not have a reason to rejoice for attending such an extravagant affair? If you knew there were storehouses of gold and the palace gates were opening at 12a.m., wouldn't you be the first to arrive, to make sure you could grab the most precious gems? It is said that Torah study for even a short time during these hours is equivalent to many hours of daytime study. This is one of the reasons why.

There are certain holidays when this prayer service is halted. Tikkun Rachel is only said on days when *Tachanun* is said; it should not be said on days of celebration, including *Shabbos* and Festivals. Tikkun Leah, according to Ashkenazi tradition, may be said even on days when *Tachanun* is not said, including *Shabbos*, Festivals and minor holidays.

Every night, the gates of Heaven are open for increased prayer, Torah study and *hisbodedus*, Jewish meditation (See my *Sefer* Kavanos Halev, Meditations of the Heart, to learn about *hisbodidus*) It is a widely accepted custom to meditate in *hisbodidus* after reciting the *tikkun* or completing the night's Torah study.

There is also a tradition to chant songs and poems; these can be found in Tikkun Chatzos prayer books. In some books there might even be *yichudim*, *kabbalistic* repairs one can do to make up for the *Shechinah*. For my part, after saying the *tikkun* I took up the composition of musical songs. Some righteous women who didn't necessarily say the *tikkun* would arise at this special hour and complete their work around the house. As is written in Mishlei, "*Vatakom b'od lailah vatiten teref l'vetah v'chok l'na'aroteiha.*" She arises while it is still night and gives food to her household and a portion to her maidservants.

Tikkun Shechinah

The holy Tikkun Chatzos prayers were meant as a guide to connect with the *Shechinah*. Since it is an extra prayer, I don't see how it would be disrespectful to rework this service toward your comfort zone. After all, you have awoken outstandingly, while the rest of the world slumbers the night away. This is your time to live it up in the holy light of *HaShem* and the *Shechinah*. Use the time wisely.

PART SIX

TIKKUN ROCHEL AND TIKKUN LEAH

In Hebrew Script (With English translation by Breslav Research Institute)

Tikkun Rachel is only recited on days when *Tachanun* is said. "A few prayers said with concentration are better than many said without" (Shulchan Arukh. Orach Chaim 1:4). Tikkun Rachel begins with Confession of Sins.

TIKKUN RACHEL

אֱלֹהֵינוּ וֵאלֹהֵי אֲבוֹתֵינוּ, תָּבֹא לְפָנֶיךָ תְּפִלָּתֵנוּ, וְאַל תִּתְעַלַּם מִתְּחִנָּתֵנוּ, שֶׁאֵין אָנוּ עַזֵּי פָנִים וּקְשֵׁי עֹרֶף, לוֹמַר לְפָנֶיךָ יְיָ אֱלֹהֵינוּ וֵאלֹהֵי אֲבוֹתֵינוּ, צַדִּיקִים אֲנַחְנוּ וְלֹא חָטָאנוּ, אֲבָל אֲנַחְנוּ וַאֲבוֹתֵינוּ חָטָאנוּ:

Our God and God of our fathers: Let our prayer come before You, and do not hide Yourself from our entreaties. For we are not as brazen and stiff-necked as to say before You, HaShem, our God and God of our fathers, "We are righteous and have not sinned." We and our ancestors have sinned.

אָשַׁמְנוּ, בָּגַדְנוּ, גָּזַלְנוּ, דִּבַּרְנוּ דֹּפִי. הֶעֱוִינוּ, וְהִרְשַׁעְנוּ, זַדְנוּ, חָמַסְנוּ, טָפַלְנוּ שֶׁקֶר. יָעַצְנוּ רָע, כִּזַּבְנוּ, לַצְנוּ, מָרַדְנוּ, נִאַצְנוּ, סָרַרְנוּ, עָוִינוּ, פָּשַׁעְנוּ, צָרַרְנוּ, קִשִּׁינוּ עֹרֶף. רָשַׁעְנוּ, שִׁחַתְנוּ, תִּעַבְנוּ, תָּעִינוּ, תִּעְתָּעְנוּ: סַרְנוּ מִמִּצְוֹתֶיךָ וּמִמִּשְׁפָּטֶיךָ הַטּוֹבִים וְלֹא שָׁוָה לָנוּ. וְאַתָּה צַדִּיק עַל כָּל הַבָּא עָלֵינוּ, כִּי אֱמֶת עָשִׂיתָ וַאֲנַחְנוּ הִרְשָׁעְנוּ:

We are guilty;

Tikkun Shechinah

We have repaid good with bad;
We have robbed;
We have spoken slander;
We have acted wrongly to others;
We have caused others to sin;
We have sinned willfully;
We have been violent;
We have joined other sinners;
We have given wrongful advice;
We have lied;
We have mocked;
We have rebelled;
We have provoked;
We have turned from the right path;
We have transgressed;
We have openly rebelled;
We have caused harm to others;
We have been obstinate;
We have acted wickedly;
We have destroyed;
We have committed abominations;
We have strayed;
We have led others astray.

We have turned from the path of Your righteous Laws and Commandments, and we have gained nothing from it. And You have been just in everything that has befallen us, for You have acted truthfully, while we have acted wickedly. We have been wicked and sinful, which is why we have not been redeemed.

מַה נֹּאמַר לְפָנֶיךָ שׁוֹכֵן שְׁחָקִים: הֲלֹא כָל וְהַנִּגְלוֹת אַתָּה יוֹדֵעַ:

What can we say before You Who sit on High? What can we tell You Who dwell in the Heavens? You know everything, whether hidden or revealed.

אַתָּה יוֹדֵעַ רָזֵי עוֹלָם וְתַעֲלוּמוֹת סִתְרֵי כָּל חָי: אַתָּה חוֹפֵשׂ כָּל חַדְרֵי בָטֶן וּבוֹחֵן כְּלָיוֹת וָלֵב. אֵין דָּבָר נֶעְלָם מִמֶּךָּ. וְאֵין נִסְתָּר מִנֶּגֶד עֵינֶיךָ:

You know the secrets of the world and the hidden thoughts of all the living. You search the innermost chambers of the heart and test all thoughts and emotions. Nothing is hidden from You, and nothing is concealed from Your eyes.

וּבְכֵן יְהִי רָצוֹן מִלְפָנֶיךָ יְיָ אֱלֹהֵינוּ וֵאלֹהֵי אֲבוֹתֵינוּ שֶׁתְּרַחֵם עָלֵינוּ וְתִמְחוֹל לָנוּ עַל כָּל חַטֹאתֵינוּ וּתְכַפֵּר לָנוּ עַל כָּל עֲוֹנוֹתֵינוּ. וְתִמְחַל וְתִסְלַח לָנוּ עַל כָּל פְּשָׁעֵינוּ:

    Therefore, let it be Your will, HaShem, our God and God of our fathers, to forgive us for all our sins, pardon us for all our transgressions, and atone for all our willful sins.

Psalm 137

עַל נַהֲרוֹת בָּבֶל, שָׁם יָשַׁבְנוּ גַּם בָּכִינוּ, בְּזָכְרֵנוּ אֶת צִיּוֹן: עַל עֲרָבִים בְּתוֹכָהּ, תָּלִינוּ כִּנֹּרוֹתֵינוּ: כִּי שָׁם שְׁאֵלוּנוּ שׁוֹבֵינוּ דִּבְרֵי שִׁיר וְתוֹלָלֵינוּ שִׂמְחָה, שִׁירוּ לָנוּ מִשִּׁיר צִיּוֹן: אֵיךְ נָשִׁיר אֶת שִׁיר יְיָ, עַל אַדְמַת נֵכָר: אִם אֶשְׁכָּחֵךְ יְרוּשָׁלָיִם, תִּשְׁכַּח יְמִינִי: תִּדְבַּק לְשׁוֹנִי לְחִכִּי אִם לֹא אֶזְכְּרֵכִי, אִם לֹא אַעֲלֶה אֶת יְרוּשָׁלַיִם עַל רֹאשׁ שִׂמְחָתִי: זְכֹר יְיָ לִבְנֵי אֱדוֹם אֵת יוֹם יְרוּשָׁלָיִם, הָאֹמְרִים עָרוּ עָרוּ עַד הַיְסוֹד בָּהּ: בַּת בָּבֶל הַשְּׁדוּדָה, אַשְׁרֵי שֶׁיְשַׁלֶּם לָךְ אֶת גְּמוּלֵךְ שֶׁגָּמַלְתְּ לָנוּ: אַשְׁרֵי שֶׁיֹּאחֵז וְנִפֵּץ אֶת עֹלָלַיִךְ אֶל הַסָּלַע:

    By the rivers of Bavel, there we sat, and also wept, when we remembered Zion. On the willows in its midst we hung our lyres. For there our captors asked us for words of song, and our spoilers asked us for joy - Sing us one of the songs of Zion. How can we sing the song of God on alien soil? If I forget you, Yerushalayim, let my right hand forget her skill. Let my tongue cleave to the roof of my mouth if I do not remember You, if I do not set Yerushalayim above my highest joy. Remember, God, against the children of Edom the day of Yerushalayim, and how they said, "Destroy it, destroy it, to its very foundation." Daughter of Bavel - marked for devastation - happy is the one who will repay you for what you have done to us. Happy is the one who will seize and beat your little ones against the rock.

Psalm 79

מִזְמוֹר לְאָסָף, אֱלֹהִים בָּאוּ גוֹיִם| בְּנַחֲלָתֶךָ טִמְּאוּ אֶת הֵיכַל קָדְשֶׁךָ שָׂמוּ אֶת יְרוּשָׁלַיִם לְעִיִּים: נָתְנוּ אֶת נִבְלַת עֲבָדֶיךָ מַאֲכָל לְעוֹף הַשָּׁמָיִם בְּשַׂר חֲסִידֶיךָ לְחַיְתוֹ אָרֶץ: שָׁפְכוּ דָמָם| כַּמַּיִם סְבִיבוֹת יְרוּשָׁלָיִם וְאֵין קוֹבֵר: הָיִינוּ חֶרְפָּה

לְשְׁכֵנֵינוּ לַעַג וָקֶלֶס לִסְבִיבוֹתֵינוּ: עַד מָה יְיָ תֶּאֱנַף לָנֶצַח תִּבְעַר כְּמוֹ אֵשׁ קִנְאָתֶךָ: שְׁפֹךְ חֲמָתְךָ אֶל הַגּוֹיִם אֲשֶׁר לֹא יְדָעוּךָ וְעַל מַמְלָכוֹת אֲשֶׁר בְּשִׁמְךָ לֹא קָרָאוּ: כִּי אָכַל אֶת יַעֲקֹב וְאֶת נָוֵהוּ הֵשַׁמּוּ: אַל תִּזְכָּר לָנוּ עֲוֹנֹת רִאשֹׁנִים מַהֵר יְקַדְּמוּנוּ רַחֲמֶיךָ כִּי דַלּוֹנוּ מְאֹד: עָזְרֵנוּ אֱלֹהֵי יִשְׁעֵנוּ עַל דְּבַר כְּבוֹד שְׁמֶךָ וְהַצִּילֵנוּ וְכַפֵּר עַל חַטֹּאתֵינוּ לְמַעַן שְׁמֶךָ: לָמָּה| יֹאמְרוּ הַגּוֹיִם אַיֵּה אֱלֹהֵיהֶם יִוָּדַע בַּגּוֹיִם לְעֵינֵינוּ נִקְמַת דַּם עֲבָדֶיךָ הַשָּׁפוּךְ: תָּבוֹא לְפָנֶיךָ אֶנְקַת אָסִיר כְּגֹדֶל זְרוֹעֲךָ הוֹתֵר בְּנֵי תְמוּתָה: וְהָשֵׁב לִשְׁכֵנֵינוּ שִׁבְעָתַיִם אֶל חֵיקָם חֶרְפָּתָם אֲשֶׁר חֵרְפוּךָ אֲדֹנָי: וַאֲנַחְנוּ עַמְּךָ| וְצֹאן מַרְעִיתֶךָ נוֹדֶה לְּךָ לְעוֹלָם לְדֹר וָדֹר נְסַפֵּר תְּהִלָּתֶךָ:

A psalm of Asaf: O God, heathen nations have come into Your inheritance; they have defiled Your Holy Temple; they have turned Yerushalayim into heaps of stones. They have given the bodies of Your slaughtered servants as food for the birds of the sky and left the flesh of Your pious for the beasts of the earth. They have shed their blood like water all around Yerushalayim, and there is none to bury them. We have become a taunt to our neighbors, a scorn and derision to those around about us. How long, God? Will You be angry forever? How long will Your vengeful fury burn like fire? Pour out Your wrath upon the nations that do not want to know You, and on the kingdoms that have not called upon Your Name. For they have devoured Yaakov, and lay waste his habitation. Do not remember our first sins against us; let Your compassion speedily come to meet us, for we have fallen very low. Help us, O God of our salvation, for the honor of Your Name. Deliver us, and forgive our sins, for the sake of Your Name. Why should the nations say, "Where is their God?" Let Your vengeance on the nations for the bloodshed of Your servants be made manifest before our eyes. Let the groaning of the imprisoned nation come before You; in Your great power, release the bonds of those appointed to die. And pay back our neighbors sevenfold into their chests for the way they have insulted You, O God. And we, Your people and the sheep of Your pasture, will thank You for ever: we will praise from generation to generation.

Lamentations 5

זְכֹר יְיָ מֶה הָיָה לָנוּ הַבִּיטָה וּרְאֵה אֶת חֶרְפָּתֵנוּ: נַחֲלָתֵנוּ נֶהֶפְכָה לְזָרִים בָּתֵּינוּ לְנָכְרִים: יְתוֹמִים הָיִינוּ וְאֵין אָב אִמֹּתֵינוּ כְּאַלְמָנוֹת: מֵימֵינוּ בְּכֶסֶף שָׁתִינוּ עֵצֵינוּ בִּמְחִיר יָבֹאוּ: עַל צַוָּארֵנוּ נִרְדָּפְנוּ יָגַעְנוּ וְלֹא הוּנַח לָנוּ: מִצְרַיִם נָתַנּוּ יָד

אֲשׁוּר לִשְׂבֹּעַ לָחֶם: אֲבֹתֵינוּ חָטְאוּ וְאֵינָם וַאֲנַחְנוּ עֲוֹנֹתֵיהֶם סָבָלְנוּ: עֲבָדִים מָשְׁלוּ בָנוּ פֹּרֵק אֵין מִיָּדָם: בְּנַפְשֵׁנוּ נָבִיא לַחְמֵנוּ מִפְּנֵי חֶרֶב הַמִּדְבָּר: עוֹרֵנוּ כְּתַנּוּר נִכְמָרוּ מִפְּנֵי זַלְעֲפוֹת רָעָב: נָשִׁים בְּצִיּוֹן עִנּוּ בְּתֻלֹת בְּעָרֵי יְהוּדָה: שָׂרִים בְּיָדָם נִתְלוּ פְּנֵי זְקֵנִים לֹא נֶהְדָּרוּ: בַּחוּרִים טְחוֹן נָשָׂאוּ וּנְעָרִים בָּעֵץ כָּשָׁלוּ: זְקֵנִים מִשַּׁעַר שָׁבָתוּ בַּחוּרִים מִנְּגִינָתָם: שָׁבַת מְשׂוֹשׂ לִבֵּנוּ נֶהְפַּךְ לְאֵבֶל מְחוֹלֵנוּ: נָפְלָה עֲטֶרֶת רֹאשֵׁנוּ אוֹי נָא לָנוּ כִּי חָטָאנוּ: עַל זֶה הָיָה דָוֶה לִבֵּנוּ עַל אֵלֶּה חָשְׁכוּ עֵינֵינוּ: עַל הַר צִיּוֹן שֶׁשָּׁמֵם שׁוּעָלִים הִלְּכוּ בוֹ: אַתָּה יְיָ לְעוֹלָם תֵּשֵׁב כִּסְאֲךָ לְדֹר וָדוֹר: לָמָּה לָנֶצַח תִּשְׁכָּחֵנוּ תַּעַזְבֵנוּ לְאֹרֶךְ יָמִים: הֲשִׁיבֵנוּ יְיָ אֵלֶיךָ וְנָשׁוּבָה חַדֵּשׁ יָמֵינוּ כְּקֶדֶם: כִּי אִם מָאֹס מְאַסְתָּנוּ קָצַפְתָּ עָלֵינוּ עַד מְאֹד: הֲשִׁיבֵנוּ יְיָ אֵלֶיךָ וְנָשׁוּבָה חַדֵּשׁ יָמֵינוּ כְּקֶדֶם:

God, remember what has happened to us; look and see our disgrace. Our inheritance has gone to strangers, our homes to foreigners. We have become orphans without a father; our mothers are like widows. We've had to pay money to drink our own water; our own wood we've had to buy. We've been oppressed with a yoke of harsh labor: we've toiled, but none of the fruits has been left for us to reap. We've stretched out our hand to Egypt for aid, we've appealed to Assyria for bread to satisfy us. Our fathers sinned - they are no more - and we are suffering for their sins. Slaves have lorded it over us: there's no one to save us from their hands. We've had to risk our very lives to obtain our bread, due to the desert sword. Our skin burns like an oven from the ravages of hunger. They've ravaged the women of Zion and the virgins of the towns of Yehudah. Nobles have been hanged by their arms; no respect has been given to the elders. Young men have been forced to bear millstones; youths have collapsed under the weight of the wood. The elders no longer sit in judgment; the young men have ceased their singing. The joy has left our hearts; our dance has turned into mourning. The crown of our head has fallen: Woe to us, for we have sinned. For this our hearts are grieved, for these our eyes have become darkened. Because of Mount Zion, which has become desolate, a place where foxes roam. But You, God, reign eternal; Your throne is from generation to generation. Why forget us forever? Why abandon us for so long?! Bring us back to You, God, and we will repent, renew our days as of old. For even if You have utterly despised us, You have already shown us Your extreme wrath. Bring us back to You, God, and we will repent! Renew our days as of old!

Tikkun Shechinah

הַבֵּט מִשָּׁמַיִם וּרְאֵה מִזְּבוּל קָדְשְׁךָ וְתִפְאַרְתֶּךָ אַיֵּה קִנְאָתְךָ וּגְבוּרֹתֶךָ הֲמוֹן מֵעֶיךָ וְרַחֲמֶיךָ אֵלַי הִתְאַפָּקוּ: כִּי אַתָּה אָבִינוּ כִּי אַבְרָהָם לֹא יְדָעָנוּ וְיִשְׂרָאֵל לֹא יַכִּירָנוּ אַתָּה יְיָ אָבִינוּ גֹּאֲלֵנוּ מֵעוֹלָם שְׁמֶךָ: לָמָּה תַתְעֵנוּ יְיָ מִדְּרָכֶיךָ תַּקְשִׁיחַ לִבֵּנוּ מִיִּרְאָתֶךָ שׁוּב לְמַעַן עֲבָדֶיךָ שִׁבְטֵי נַחֲלָתֶךָ: לַמִּצְעָר יָרְשׁוּ עַם קָדְשֶׁךָ. צָרֵינוּ בּוֹסְסוּ מִקְדָּשֶׁךָ:

וְעַתָּה יְיָ אָבִינוּ אָתָּה אֲנַחְנוּ הַחֹמֶר וְאַתָּה יֹצְרֵנוּ וּמַעֲשֵׂה יָדְךָ כֻּלָּנוּ: אַל תִּקְצֹף יְיָ עַד מְאֹד וְאַל לָעַד תִּזְכֹּר עָוֹן הֵן הַבֶּט נָא עַמְּךָ כֻלָּנוּ: עָרֵי קָדְשְׁךָ הָיוּ מִדְבָּר צִיּוֹן מִדְבָּר הָיָתָה יְרוּשָׁלַיִם שְׁמָמָה: בֵּית קָדְשֵׁנוּ וְתִפְאַרְתֵּנוּ אֲשֶׁר הִלְלוּךָ אֲבֹתֵינוּ הָיָה לִשְׂרֵפַת אֵשׁ וְכָל מַחֲמַדֵּינוּ הָיָה לְחָרְבָּה: הַעַל אֵלֶּה תִתְאַפַּק יְיָ תֶּחֱשֶׁה וּתְעַנֵּנוּ עַד מְאֹד:

הַטֵּה אֱלֹהַי אָזְנְךָ וּשְׁמָע פְּקַח עֵינֶיךָ וּרְאֵה שֹׁמְמֹתֵינוּ וְהָעִיר אֲשֶׁר נִקְרָא שִׁמְךָ עָלֶיהָ: כִּי לֹא עַל צִדְקֹתֵינוּ, אֲנַחְנוּ מַפִּילִים תַּחֲנוּנֵינוּ לְפָנֶיךָ כִּי עַל רַחֲמֶיךָ הָרַבִּים: אֲדֹנָי שְׁמָעָה אֲדֹנָי סְלָחָה אֲדֹנָי הַקְשִׁיבָה וַעֲשֵׂה אַל תְּאַחַר לְמַעֲנְךָ אֱלֹהַי כִּי שִׁמְךָ נִקְרָא עַל עִירְךָ וְעַל עַמֶּךָ:

    Look down from Heaven and see from Your palace of holiness and glory: where is Your vengeance and Your might? Your abundant compassion and love for me have been withheld. For You are our Father - for Avraham did not know us, nor does Israel recognize us. You, God, are our Father, our Redeemer: Your Name is eternal. God, why do You make us stray from Your ways? Why do You harden our hearts against revering You? Come back to us, for the sake of Your servants, the tribes whom You made, Your portion. Only for a short while did Your holy nation inherit our land: our oppressors trampled Your Holy Temple (Isaiah 63:15-18).

    And now, God, You are our Father. We are the material and You are our Maker. We are all the work of Your hands. Do not be exceedingly angry with us, God. Do not remember our transgression forever. Please see - we are all Your people. Your holy cities have become wastelands. Zion has become a desert, Yerushalayim is desolate. The house of our holiness and glory, where our forefathers praised You, has been burned down by fire. Everything we cherished has become a ruin. Can You restrain Yourself over all this, God? Will You remain silent, and let our extreme suffering continue? (ibid. 64:7-11).

הֲמָאֹס מָאַסְתָּ אֶת יְהוּדָה, אִם בְּצִיּוֹן גָּעֲלָה נַפְשֶׁךָ, מַדּוּעַ הִכִּיתָנוּ וְאֵין לָנוּ מַרְפֵּא, קַוֵּה לְשָׁלוֹם וְאֵין טוֹב, וּלְעֵת מַרְפֵּא וְהִנֵּה בְעָתָה: יָדַעְנוּ אֲדֹנָי רִשְׁעֵנוּ, עֲוֹן אֲבוֹתֵינוּ, כִּי חָטָאנוּ לָךְ: אַל תִּנְאַץ לְמַעַן שִׁמְךָ, אַל תְּנַבֵּל כִּסֵּא כְבוֹדֶךָ, זְכֹר, אַל תָּפֵר בְּרִיתְךָ אִתָּנוּ:

Have You completely despised Yehudah? Is Your soul repulsed by Zion? Why have You struck us with afflictions for which we can find no cure? We hope for peace, but we see no good. When we expected healing, we were stricken with dread. We know our wickedness, God, and the sin of our ancestors, for we have sinned against You. For the sake of Your Name, don't humiliate us. Don't disgrace Your Throne of Glory. Remember Your covenant with us - don't violate it (Jeremiah 14:19-21).

כֹּה אָמַר אֲדֹנָי קוֹל בְּרָמָה נִשְׁמָע, נְהִי בְּכִי תַמְרוּרִים, רָחֵל מְבַכָּה עַל בָּנֶיהָ, מֵאֲנָה לְהִנָּחֵם עַל בָּנֶיהָ כִּי אֵינֶנּוּ: (ירמיה פרק לא יד), אֲדֹנָי מִמָּרוֹם יִשְׁאָג וּמִמְּעוֹן קָדְשׁוֹ יִתֵּן קוֹלוֹ שָׁאֹג יִשְׁאַג עַל נָוֵהוּ (ירמיה פרק כה ל), וַיִּקְרָא אֲדֹנָי יֱהֹוִה צְבָאוֹת בַּיּוֹם הַהוּא לִבְכִי וּלְמִסְפֵּד וּלְקָרְחָה וְלַחֲגֹר שָׂק: (ישעיה פרק כב), עַל אֵלֶּה אֲנִי בוֹכִיָּה עֵינִי עֵינִי יֹרְדָה מַּיִם כִּי רָחַק מִמֶּנִּי מְנַחֵם מֵשִׁיב נַפְשִׁי, הָיוּ בָנַי שׁוֹמֵמִים כִּי גָבַר אוֹיֵב (איכה פרק א טז), הֵן אֶרְאֶלָּם צָעֲקוּ חֻצָה, מַלְאֲכֵי שָׁלוֹם מַר יִבְכָּיוּן: (ישעיה פרק לג ז).

Thus, said God: A voice is heard on High, a lament, bitter weeping. Rachel cries for her children. She refuses to be comforted, for they are gone (ibid. 31:14). God roars from on High, and from the place of His holiness He lets out His cry. He roars and roars over His habitation (ibid. 25:30). On that day the Lord God of Hosts called for wailing and mourning, the tearing of hair and the donning of sackcloth (Isaiah 22:12). For these I weep. My eye! My eye pours forth water. For my comforter, the one who will restore my soul is far from me. My children are devastated, because the enemy has been so strong (Lamentations 1:16). Even the angels cried on the streets; the messengers of peace weep bitterly (Isaiah 33:7).

Tikkun Shechinah

*

It is customary to recite the following five laments.

The First Lament, by Rabbi Moshe Alshikh

הִקָּבְצוּ וְשִׁמְעוּ בְּנֵי יַעֲקֹב כֻּלְּכֶם. קִרְעוּ לְבַבְכֶם וְאַל בִּגְדֵיכֶם. כִּי בְפִשְׁעֵיכֶם שֻׁלְּחָה אִמְּכֶם. וּתְנוּ כָבוֹד לַאֲדֹנָי אֱלֹהֵיכֶם:

Gather and listen, all of you children of Yaakov. Tear your hearts, not your clothes! Because of your sins your mother has been cast out. Give due honor to HaShem your God.

מִי הָאִישׁ הֶחָפֵץ חַיִּים וְחַךְ אֹכֶל יִטְעַם לוֹ. אֹהֵב יָמִים לִרְאוֹת טוֹב וּלְבַקֵּר בְּהֵיכָלוֹ. וְהָאֱלֹהִים יִרְאֶה לוֹ לִשְׁכֹּן בְּאָהֳלוֹ מִבְּלִי לוֹ. אֲשֶׁר לֹא עָמַל בּוֹ וְלֹא גִדְּלוֹ:

Who is the man who wants life? Who wants to enjoy the taste of his food? How can anyone think about enjoying his life and leading a peaceful existence in his home while God Himself allows strangers to dwell in His Sanctuary, aliens whom He did not struggle to raise?

אָנָה הָלַךְ דּוֹדֵךְ תַּרְקִיעַ עִמּוֹ לַשְּׁחָקִים. אָנֹכִי חָטָאתִי וְהוּא אָסוּר בַּזִּקִּים וְעַל זֹאת סִפְדוּ וְהֵילִילוּ בֹּאוּ וְלִינוּ בַשַּׂקִּים. בָּרְחוֹבוֹת וּבַשְּׁוָקִים:

Where has your Beloved gone? Can you fly with Him to the heavens?" [Israel replies]: "I have sinned, and He is bound in chains. And for this, grieve and wail; go and lie in sackcloth in the streets and marketplaces.

שְׁכִינָה מָה אוֹמֶרֶת קַלַּנִי מֵרֹאשִׁי. הַגְּדֻלָּה וְהַגְּבוּרָה וְהַתִּפְאֶרֶת עָבְרוּ רֹאשִׁי. וְהַנֵּצַח וְהַהוֹד אֵין דּוֹרֵשׁ לְנַפְשִׁי. וַתִּזְנַח מִשָּׁלוֹם נַפְשִׁי:

What does the *Shechinah* say? "Ay! My head! The greatness, might and glory have departed from My head. Gone are the triumph and the splendor. No one is concerned with my soul. My soul is despised and finds no peace."

עַל זֹאת אֶסְפְּדָה וְאֵילִילָה. אֲסַלְּדָה בְחִילָה. קוֹלִי כַּחוֹלָה. מֵעַי מֵעַי אוֹחִילָה. לְמַעַנְכֶם שֻׁלַּחְתִּי בָּבֶלָה. וַאֲנִי בְּתוֹךְ הַגּוֹלָה:

For this I mourn and wail. I am feverish with dread. I scream like a woman in labor from the agonizing pain in my belly. Because of you I was banished to Bavel, and am deep in exile.

עֲוֹנוֹתֵיכֶם הִטּוּ אֵלֶּה וְחַטֹּאתֵיכֶם. הִגְלֵיתִי אֶתְכֶם לְיַסְּרָה אֶתְכֶם. וַיִּתְעַבֵּר אֲדֹנָי בִּי לְמַעֲנְכֶם. וַיִּשְׁלָחֵנִי אֱלֹהִים לִפְנֵיכֶם:

Your sins and wrongdoing caused of all this. Together we were exiled that I may torment you. God was enraged with me because of you, and sent me ahead of you.

בְּבֵית יִשְׂרָאֵל רָאִיתִי שַׁעֲרוּרִיָּה. אֵין אִישׁ שָׂם עַל לֵב שֶׁלְּמָּה אֶהְיֶה כְּעוֹטְיָה. כְּקִיר נָטוּי וּכְגָדֵר הַדְּחוּיָה. הֲמִדְבָּר הָיִיתִי לְיִשְׂרָאֵל אִם אֶרֶץ מַאְפֵּלְיָה:

I have seen something shameful in the House of Israel: nobody takes to heart that I am forced to wander. I am like a tottering wall, a fence about to collapse. Was I a desert or a dark wasteland to Israel?

יָדַעְנוּ אֲדֹנָי רִשְׁעֵנוּ, וַעֲוֹן אֲבוֹתֵינוּ. הִנְנוּ אָתָאנוּ, לְךָ אֲדֹנָי אֱלֹהֵינוּ. שׁוּב לְמַעַן עֲבָדֶיךָ, וּסְלַח תְּפָּא לַעֲוֹנֵנוּ. תָּשׁוּב תְּרַחֲמֵנוּ, וְתִכְבּשׁ עֲוֹנוֹתֵינוּ:

O God, we acknowledge our wickedness and the sins of our fathers. We hereby repent HaShem, our God. Return for the sake of Your servants and forgive our transgressions. Return! Have pity on us and pay no attention to our sins.

וַיֹּאמֶר אֲדֹנָי אֲהַבְתִּי אֶתְכֶם. כָּל יִשְׁעִי וְכָל חֵפְצִי אָשׁוּב לְרַחֲמְכֶם. שׁוּבוּ אֵלַי וְאָשׁוּבָה אֲלֵיכֶם. אָנֹכִי אָנֹכִי הוּא מְנַחֶמְכֶם:

God says: "I love you. My sole intent, My only desire is to return from my anger and to have compassion on you. Return to Me and I will return to you. I, only I, am your Consoler."

וַיֹּאמֶר אֲדֹנָי אֲהַבְתִּי אֶתְכֶם. כָּל יִשְׁעִי וְכָל חֵפְצִי אָשׁוּב לְרַחֲמְכֶם. שׁוּבוּ אֵלַי וְאָשׁוּבָה אֲלֵיכֶם. אָנֹכִי אָנֹכִי הוּא מְנַחֶמְכֶם:

Tell the daughter of Zion, thus says your Master; "Instead of your being abandoned like a widow any more, your sons will now return to you. And as a groom delights in his bride, so will your God delight in you. And you will be a crown of glory in the hand of God and a royal diadem in the palm of God."

The Second Lament, by Rabbi Chaim HaKohen

קוֹל בָּרָמָה נִשְׁמָע בִּילָלָה. קוֹל נְהִי מִצִּיּוֹן הַמְהֻלָּלָה: קוֹל ברמה:

A voice is heard wailing on High, the voice of lamentation from the illustrious city of Zion.

חָשַׁבְתִּי יָמִים הָיִיתִי גְבֶרֶת. בְּיַד אֲדֹנָי עֲטֶרֶת תִּפְאָרֶת. וְעַתָּה אֲנִי שֶׁחַרְחֹרֶת. טָבַעְתִּי בְּבוֹר בְּיָוֵן מְצוּלָה: קוֹל:

I remember back to the days when I was mistress, a crown of glory in the hand of God. But now I am darkened. I've sunk in a pit, down into the muddy depths. *A voice...*

יְחִידָה רַעְיָה אֲזַי הָיִיתִי. וּכְבוֹד עֶלְיוֹן אֲנִי נִקְרֵאתִי. וְעַתָּה לְתַחְתִּיּוֹת יָרַדְתִּי. וְדוֹדִי וְרֵעִי לָרוּם עָלָה: קוֹל:

Back then I was His sole beloved, and I was called, "The glory of the Supreme One." But now I've descended to the depths, while my dear Beloved has ascended to the heights. *A voice...*

יַחַד יוֹדְעַי בְּתוּלוֹתַי וְרֵעְיוֹתַי. בְּכוּ נָא עִמִּי כִּי רַבּוֹת אֲנְחוֹתַי. אֵין נוֹטֶה עוֹד אָהֳלִי וּמֵקִים יְרִיעוֹתַי. כִּי דוֹדִי מֶנִּי נָסַע וְנִגְלָה: קוֹל:

My friends, my maidens, my dear ones: together, weep with me. I have so much to mourn for. There is no one to pitch my tent or hang my curtains. For my Beloved has left me. He is exiled. *A voice...*

מִמָּרוֹם הֻשְׁלַכְתִּי בְּרֹב מְגִנָּה. שָׁלַח אֵשׁ בְּעַצְמוֹתַי וַיִּרְדֶּנָּה. וְיָצָאתִי בַּגּוֹלָה בָּדָד כְּאַלְמָנָה. הָגְלָה יְהוּדָה הָגְלַת שְׁלוֹמִים כֻּלָּהּ: קוֹל:

From above I was cast down in great distress. He has sent fire into my bones to break them. I've gone out into exile, forlorn as a widow. The exile was total: the entire land of Yehudah was exiled. *A voice...*

הָיִיתִי כְכַלָּה בְּתוֹךְ אַפִּרְיוֹן. וַעֲנַן יוֹמָם עַל מְכוֹן הַר צִיּוֹן. הֻשְׁלַכְתִּי לַחוּץ כְּעָנִי וְאֶבְיוֹן. בִּגְדִי לָקַח צָר וַאֲנִי אֻמְלָלָה: קוֹל:

I was like a bride under her canopy. God's cloud stood daily over Mount Zion. Then I was thrown outside like a beggar and a pauper. My foe has snatched my clothes. How wretched am I! *A voice...*

כֹּהֲנַי וּזְקֵנַי טָבְחוּ אוֹיְבַי. מַחֲזִיקִים בִּבְרִיתִי זֶרַע אוֹהֲבַי. בָּנַי הַיְקָרִים וּבַחוּרַי. הָלְכוּ בַשְּׁבִי וְעוֹלָלַי בַּגּוֹלָה: קוֹל:

My enemies slaughtered my priests and elders, those who adhered to my covenant, the seed of my love ones [the patriarchs]. My cherished sons and youths have been taken captive. My little children are in exile. *A voice...*

הֵן כָּל אֵלֶּה אֵין דּוֹרֵשׁ לְנַפְשִׁי. אֻמְלָּאָה הֶחָרְבָה וְאֵל עַמִּים אָרִים רֹאשִׁי. וְאוֹיְבִי אָמַר לֹא תִּקְרְאִי עוֹד אִישִׁי. כִּי נָפַלְתִּי לִפְנֵי בְנֵי עַוְלָה: קוֹל:

After all this, there's still no one to plead my cause and help me regain my ascendancy and lift my head to the nations. My enemy says, "No more will you call God 'my husband,' for I have fallen into the hands of evildoers." *A voice...*

נָא אָב הָרַחֲמָן תָּשׁוּב לְצִיּוֹן. עַיִן בְּעַיִן נִרְאֶה בְּבִנְיַן אַפִּרְיוֹן. וְהַבַּיִת הַזֶּה יִהְיֶה עֶלְיוֹן. וְאָז גְּאוּלִים יִפְצְחוּ צְהָלָה: וְהַבַּיִת הַזֶּה יִהְיֶה עֶלְיוֹן. וְאָז גְּאוּלִים יִפְצְחוּ צְהָלָה:

Please, merciful Father, return to Zion, so that we may witness with our eyes the rebuilding of Your Sanctuary, and this [third] house will be supreme. Then the redeemed Ones will shout for joy. *And this third house will be Supreme...*

The Third Lament, from Yerushalayim, author unknown

For how long, God, must Your nation weep before You on this day over Your House of Prayer, which Your enemies have burned, killing the children of Your covenant? *God! Heathens have entered Your Sanctuary!*	עַד מָתַי אֲדֹנָי בְּיוֹם זֶה לְעֻמָּתָךְ. בַּמֶּה תִּיַלֵּל עֲדָתָךְ. עַל בֵּית תְּפִלָּתָךְ. אֲשֶׁר שָׂרְפוּ צָרֶיךָ. וְהָרְגוּ בְּנֵי בְרִיתָךְ. אֱלֹהִים בָּאוּ גוֹיִם בְּנַחֲלָתָךְ
For how long, God, will You forget the uproar of those who have risen up against You, and the devastation of Your Temple? For how long will You ignore the dispersal of Your nation, who suffer for Your sake	עַד מָתַי אֲדֹנָי בְּיוֹם זֶה לְעֻמָּתָךְ. בַּמֶּה תִּיַלֵּל עֲדָתָךְ. עַל בֵּית תְּפִלָּתָךְ. אֲשֶׁר שָׂרְפוּ צָרֶיךָ. וְהָרְגוּ בְּנֵי בְרִיתָךְ

Tikkun Shechinah

and are martyred for the sake of Your Name?	
How long will You angrily reject the prayers of Your nation, who lament before You over the destruction of Your house? *God! Heathens have entered Your Sanctuary!*	עַד מָתַי עָשַׁנְתָּ בִּתְפִלַּת עַמֶּךָ. אֲשֶׁר יֶהֱגוּ לְפָנֶיךָ עַל חֻרְבַּן בֵּיתֶךָ. אֱלֹהִים בָּאוּ גוֹיִם בְּנַחֲלָתֶךָ
For how long, God, must I lie amidst the furnaces? Between the oven and the stove, my eyes are blinded. Those who burn me are keen on their work, morning, noon and night.	עַד מָתַי אֲדֹנָי אֶשְׁכְּבָה בֵּין שְׁפַתָּיִם. וּבֵין תַּנּוּר וְכִירָיִם. יְכְהוּ לִי עֵינָיִם. לוֹהֲטִים לִי יִשְׁאֲפוּ עֶרֶב וָבֹקֶר וְצָהֳרָיִם
For how long must I bear the ruin of double destruction? For how long will You withhold Your mercy from Yerushalayim? For how long must the remnant of Your flock mourn over their pain? *God! Heathens have entered Your Sanctuary!*	עַד מָתַי אֶשְׁתּוֹמֵם עַל חֻרְבָּן פַּעֲמָיִם. עַד מָתַי לֹא תְרַחֵם אֶת יְרוּשָׁלָיִם: עַד מָתַי יֶהֱגוּ בְּצַר שְׁאֵרִית צֹאן מַרְעִיתֶךָ. אֱלֹהִים בָּאוּ גוֹיִם בְּנַחֲלָתֶךָ
For how long, God, will the wicked nations rejoice - those who consumed Yaakov and humiliate him at every opportunity? I seek their welfare, but they tear out my hair. They shame me, beat my jaws, and then curl their lips in disdain.	עַד מָתַי אֲדֹנָי עכו"ם יַעֲלֹזוּ. אֲשֶׁר אָכַל אֶת יַעֲקֹב וּבְכָל עֵת יָבוֹזוּ. אֲנִי אֶדְרֹשׁ אֶת שְׁלוֹמָם וְהֵם יִמְרְטוּ וְיָגֹזּוּ. בְּחֶרְפָּה הִכּוּ לְחָיַי וּבְשִׂפְתֵי שָׁוְא נָלוֹזוּ
For how long, God, will the wicked rejoice? Until when must I [one's own name], the son of [one's mother's name] Your maidservant wail in captivity? *God! Heathens have entered Your Sanctuary!*	ד מָתַי אֲדֹנָי רְשָׁעִים יַעֲלֹזוּ. עַד אָן יִצְעַק בַּשֶּׁבִי (פלוני בן פלונית) אֲמָתֶךָ. אֱלֹהִים בָּאוּ גוֹיִם בְּנַחֲלָתֶךָ

The Fourth Lament, author unknown

In Your temple grow thorns	בְּהֵיכָלֵךְ שָׁמִיר וָשַׁיִת. הִנֵּה זֹאת

and thistles. This was the fate of the House.	תּוֹרַת הַבַּיִת: בהיכלך:
How could the Sanctuary have been laid waste and the foundation of the world destroyed? The stars and their brilliance became dimmed, as the Master of the House left.	אֵיכָה נֶחֱרַב הָאוּלָם. וְנֶהֱרַס יְסוֹד הָעוֹלָם. וְחָלוּ כּוֹכָבִים וְהָלָם. ויצא הכהן מן הבית ובא אשר לו הַבַּיִת:בהיכלך:
The Holy Dwelling that You built to bestow upon the nation You acquired... Oy! For You instructed the enemies to come and empty the House!	דִּירַת קֹדֶשׁ אֲשֶׁר בָּנִיתָ. לְהַנְחִיל לְעַם זוּ קָנִיתָ. אוֹי כִּי הָאוֹיְבִים צִוִּיתָ. יָבֹאוּ וּפִנּוּ אֶת הַבַּיִת: בהיכלך:
All her lights were darkened, all her gates were closed. Until all who saw it said, "There appears to be a leprous mark on the House."	נֶחְשְׁכוּ כָּל מְאוֹרֶיהָ. סֻגְּרוּ כָּל שְׁעָרֶיהָ. עַד כִּי אָמְרוּ כָּל רוֹאֶיהָ. כְּנֶגַע נִרְאָה לִי בַּבָּיִת: בהיכלך:
God! Cease Your anger and Your wrath. Remember the words of Your prophecy: To make known to Your people how great will be the glory of the House!	אֲדֹנָי שׁוּב מֵחֲרוֹן אַפְּךָ וַחֲמָתְךָ. וּזְכֹר דְּבַר נְבוּאָתְךָ. לְבַשֵּׂר נָא לְעֲדָתְךָ. גָּדוֹל יִהְיֶה כְּבוֹד הַבַּיִת לבשר נא וכו: (חגי ב ט)

A Lament by Rabbi Yaakov of Emden (the Ya'avetz)

Woe to me for the exile of the *Shechinah*!	אוֹי לִי עַל גָּלוּת הַשְּׁכִינָה
Woe to me for the destruction of the Temple!	אוֹי לִי עַל חָרְבָן ביהמ"ק
Woe to me for the burning of *Torah* scrolls!	אוֹי לִי עַל שְׂרֵפַת הַתּוֹרָה
Woe to me for the murder of *tzaddikim*!	אוֹי לִי עַל הֲרִיגַת הַצַּדִּיקִים

Woe to me for the desecration of God's Holy Name and His holy <u>Torah</u>!	אוֹי לִי עַל חִילוּל שְׁמוֹ הַגָּדוֹל וְתוֹרָתוֹ הַקְדוֹשָׁה
Woe to me for the power of the enemy!	אוֹי לִי עַל כִּי גָבַר אוֹיֵב
Woe to me for the little children who study <u>Torah</u>, who are gone!	אוֹי לִי עַל תִּינוֹקוֹת שֶׁל בֵּית רַבָּן שֶׁבָּטְלוּ
Woe to me for the anguish of all the worlds!	אוֹי לִי עַל צַעַר כָּל הָעוֹלָמוֹת
Woe to me for the suffering of the Patriarchs and Matriarchs!	אוֹי לִי עַל צַעַר הָאָבוֹת הַקְדוֹשִׁים וְהָאִמָהוֹת הַקְדוֹשׁוֹת
Woe to me for the suffering of the prophets, the *tzaddikim* and the righteous in *Gan Eden*!	אוֹי לִי עַל צַעַר הַנְבִיאִים וְהַחֲסִידִים וְהַצַדִיקִים אֲשֶׁר בג"ע
Woe to me for the pain of Mashiach!	אוֹי לִי עַל צַעֲרוֹ שֶׁל מָשִׁיחַ
Our iniquities have caused this suffering, our rebellion has lengthened our exile and our sins have kept us from good.	עֲוֹנוֹתֵינוּ הִטוּ אֵלֶה וּפְשָׁעֵינוּ הֶאֱרִיכוּ קִצֵנוּ וְחַטֹּאתֵינוּ מָנְעוּ הַטוֹב מִמֶנוּ
Woe to the children who have been exiled from their Father's table. How many bad days and years have passed since the Temple was destroyed!	אוֹי לָהֶם לַבָּנִים שֶׁגָלוּ מֵעַל שֻׁלְחָן אֲבִיהֶם זֶה כַּמָה אוֹרֶךְ יָמִים וְשָׁנִים רַבִּים וְרָעִים
Every generation, in which the Temple is not rebuilt, it is as if it was destroyed in that generation.	וְכָל דוֹר שֶׁלֹא נִבְנָה ביהמ"ק בְּיָמָיו כְּאִילוּ נֶחֱרַב בְּיָמָיו.

The Fifth Lament, author unknown

For my sanctuary I weep day and night, and for the glory of Zion, the celebrated city. A constant weeping for the double destruction, for the precious land of Israel, for Yerushalayim	עַל הֵיכָלִי אֶבְכֶּה יוֹמָם וָלָיְלָה. וּלְתִפְאֶרֶת צִיוֹן עִיר הַמְהֻלָלָה: בְּכִי תָמִיד עַל הַחֻרְבָּן פַּעֲמָיִם. אֶרֶץ צְבִי וִירוּשָׁלַיִם. וְעַל עַמָה אֲשֶׁר הָלְכוּ בַגוֹלָה: ולתפארת

and for her nation, who have gone into exile. And for the glory of Zion, the celebrated city.	
The enemy has lain waste my House of Glory. He delivered me into the hands of Nevayot [son of Ishmael] and Shama [descendant of Esav]. For this I weep constantly. I mourn and wail. And for the glory of Zion, the celebrated city.	בֵּית תִּפְאַרְתִּי שָׁם אוֹיֵב לְשַׁמָּה. הוֹשִׁיבַנִי בִּידֵי נְבָיוֹת וְשַׁמָּה. עַל זֹאת אֶבְכֶּה תָּמִיד בְּקוֹל יְלָלָה. ולתפארת :
Lament, O <u>Torah</u>, for your glory has been defiled. Your crown has fallen since the day your house was destroyed. For this I lament for Yerushalayim and Shomron. And for the glory of Zion, the celebrated city.	סִפְדִי תוֹרָה כִּי חֻלְּלָה תִפְאַרְתֵּךְ. נָפְלָה נִזְרֵךְ מִיּוֹם שֶׁחָרַב בֵּיתֵךְ. עַל זֹאת אֶשָּׂא קִינָה עַל אָהֳלִיבָה וְאָהֳלָה: ולתפארת:
Strengthen yourselves, My people. I will soon build your Sanctuary. I will clothe Myself in revenge and bring back your captives. I will dwell in My Temple as at first. For <u>Torah</u> and praise will come forth from Zion, as it is written (Isaiah 2:3), "For from Zion shall come forth <u>Torah</u> and the word of God from Yerushalayim."	חִזְקִי עַמִּי מַהֵר אֶבְנֶה לְבִירְכֶם. נָקָם אַלְבִּישׁ וְאָשִׁיב אֶת שְׁבוּתְכֶם. תּוֹךְ הֵיכָלִי אֶשְׁכּוֹן כְּבַתְּחִלָּה. כִּי מִצִּיּוֹן תֵּצֵא תוֹרָה וּתְהִלָּה. כַּדִּכְתִיב כִּי מִצִּיּוֹן תֵּצֵא תוֹרָה וּדְבַר אֲדֹנָי מִירוּשָׁלָיִם: (ישעיהו ב ג ומיכה ד' ב')
Please arouse Your exalted right arm, and call the one who has suffered Your anger "The comforted one." And let the poor, wretched people, who have been so afflicted and storm-tossed, be told: "Take comfort!"	עוּרָה נָא יְמִינְךָ רָמָה. וְלַזְעוּמָה קְרָא נֶחָמָה. וְיֵאָמֵר לְעַם דַּלָּה וַעֲגוּמָה. עֲנִיָּה סֹעֲרָה רֻחָמָה:
Please awaken! Bare Your arm and let Your final salvation be	עוּרָה נָא חֲשׂוֹף זְרוֹעֶךָ. וְיִגָּלֶה קֵץ יִשְׁעֶךָ.

revealed! And let the silent lamb that has been so afflicted and storm-tossed be told: "Take comfort!"	וְיֹאמַר לְשֶׂה נֶאֱלָמָה. עֲנִיָּה סֹעֲרָה רֻחָמָה:
Please arouse Your right arm, O God, and redeem Israel in Your mercy. And let the impoverished, begging nation be told: "The Redeemer has come to Zion."	עוּרָה נָא יְמִינְךָ הָאֵל. וּפְדֵה בְּרַחֲמֶיךָ יִשְׂרָאֵל. וְיֹאמַר לְעַם דַּל הַשּׁוֹאֵל. וּבָא לְצִיּוֹן גּוֹאֵל:
Please arouse Your right arm, Highest One! Build Zion in Your mercy. And let the poor, impoverished nation be told: "God has comforted Zion!" As it is written (Isaiah 51:3), "For God has comforted Zion. He has comforted all her desolate places, and made her deserts like Eden and her wilderness like the garden of God. Joy and happiness will be found there, thanksgiving and the sound of song."	עוּרָה נָא יְמִינְךָ עֶלְיוֹן. וּבְנֵה בְּרַחֲמֶיךָ אֶת צִיּוֹן. וְיֹאמַר לְעַם דַּל וְאֶבְיוֹן. כִּי נִחַם אֲדֹנָי צִיּוֹן. כַּדִּכְתִיב (ישעיה נא ג) כִּי נִחַם אֲדֹנָי צִיּוֹן נִחַם כָּל חָרְבֹתֶיהָ וַיָּשֶׂם מִדְבָּרָהּ כְּעֵדֶן וְעַרְבָתָהּ כְּגַן אֲדֹנָי שָׂשׂוֹן וְשִׂמְחָה יִמָּצֵא בָהּ תּוֹדָה וְקוֹל זִמְרָה:

After reciting the laments, one rises and recites the following verses of comfort:

הִתְנַעֲרִי מֵעָפָר קוּמִי שְּׁבִי יְרוּשָׁלָםִ, הִתְפַּתְּחִי מוֹסְרֵי צַוָּארֵךְ שְׁבִיָּה בַּת צִיּוֹן:
Shake the dust off yourself. Arise and be seated, Yerushalayim. Free yourself from the bonds around your neck, captive daughter of Zion (Isaiah 52:2).

עַל חוֹמֹתַיִךְ יְרוּשָׁלַםִ הִפְקַדְתִּי שֹׁמְרִים כָּל הַיּוֹם וְכָל הַלַּיְלָה תָּמִיד לֹא יֶחֱשׁוּ הַמַּזְכִּרִים אֶת אֲדֹנָי אַל דֳּמִי לָכֶם: וְאַל תִּתְּנוּ דֳמִי לוֹ עַד יְכוֹנֵן וְעַד יָשִׂים אֶת יְרוּשָׁלַםִ תְּהִלָּה בָּאָרֶץ: נִשְׁבַּע אֲדֹנָי בִּימִינוֹ וּבִזְרוֹעַ עֻזּוֹ אִם אֶתֵּן אֶת דְּגָנֵךְ עוֹד מַאֲכָל לְאֹיְבַיִךְ וְאִם יִשְׁתּוּ בְנֵי נֵכָר תִּירוֹשֵׁךְ אֲשֶׁר יָגַעַתְּ בּוֹ: כִּי מְאַסְפָיו יֹאכְלֻהוּ וְהִלְלוּ אֶת אֲדֹנָי וּמְקַבְּצָיו יִשְׁתֻּהוּ בְּחַצְרוֹת קָדְשִׁי:

I have set watchmen on your walls day and night, Yerushalayim: they will never be silent, nor cease reminding God. Don't be silent, and don't allow Him to rest until He establishes Yerushalayim and makes her exalted on earth. God has sworn by His right hand and His mighty arm: No more will I let your grain be food for your enemies, nor will strangers drink your wine, for which you have toiled. Those who harvest it will eat it and praise God. Those who gather it in will drink it in the courtyards of My holy place (ibid. 62: 6-9).

הַטֵּה אֱלֹהַי אָזְנְךָ וּשְׁמָע פְּקַח עֵינֶיךָ וּרְאֵה שֹׁמְמֹתֵינוּ וְהָעִיר אֲשֶׁר נִקְרָא שִׁמְךָ עָלֶיהָ כִּי לֹא עַל צִדְקֹתֵינוּ אֲנַחְנוּ מַפִּילִים תַּחֲנוּנֵינוּ לְפָנֶיךָ כִּי עַל רַחֲמֶיךָ הָרַבִּים: אֲדֹנָי שְׁמָעָה אֲדֹנָי סְלָחָה אֲדֹנָי הַקְשִׁיבָה וַעֲשֵׂה אַל תְּאַחַר לְמַעֲנְךָ אֱלֹהַי כִּי שִׁמְךָ נִקְרָא עַל עִירְךָ וְעַל עַמֶּךָ: (דניאל פרק ט,יח-יט), אַתָּה תָקוּם תְּרַחֵם צִיּוֹן, כִּי עֵת לְחֶנְנָהּ כִּי בָא מוֹעֵד: כִּי רָצוּ עֲבָדֶיךָ אֶת אֲבָנֶיהָ וְאֶת עֲפָרָהּ יְחֹנֵנוּ: (תהילים פרק קב,יד-טו), בּוֹנֵה יְרוּשָׁלַיִם אֲדֹנָי, נִדְחֵי יִשְׂרָאֵל יְכַנֵּס: (תהילים פרק קמז,ב)

Turn Your ear, my God, and listen. Open Your eyes and see our barren places and the city which bears Your Name. For we do not rely upon our righteousness in our petition to You, only upon Your abundant mercy. God, hear! God, forgive! Listen, and act. Do not delay - for Your sake, my God, for Your city and Your people bear Your Name (Daniel 9:18-19).

You will arise and have mercy on Zion. For it is time to have pity on her. Surely the time has come. For Your servants desire her stages; her very dust is very dear to them (Psalms 102:14-15). God is the builder of Yerushalayim. He will gather in the dispersed of Israel (ibid. 147:2)

TIKKUN LEAH

Tikkun Leah is recited even on days when Tachanun is not said. If you are saying just the Tikkun Leah, say the initial paragraphs from Tikkun Rachel.

Psalm 24

לְדָוִד מִזְמוֹר, לַאֲדֹנָי הָאָרֶץ וּמְלוֹאָהּ, תֵּבֵל וְיֹשְׁבֵי בָהּ: כִּי הוּא עַל יַמִּים יְסָדָהּ וְעַל נְהָרוֹת יְכוֹנְנֶהָ: מִי יַעֲלֶה בְהַר אֲדֹנָי וּמִי יָקוּם בִּמְקוֹם קָדְשׁוֹ: נְקִי כַפַּיִם וּבַר לֵבָב אֲשֶׁר לֹא נָשָׂא לַשָּׁוְא נַפְשִׁי וְלֹא נִשְׁבַּע לְמִרְמָה: יִשָּׂא בְרָכָה מֵאֵת אֲדֹנָי וּצְדָקָה מֵאֱלֹהֵי יִשְׁעוֹ: זֶה דּוֹר דֹּרְשָׁיו מְבַקְשֵׁי פָנֶיךָ יַעֲקֹב סֶלָה: שְׂאוּ שְׁעָרִים רָאשֵׁיכֶם וְהִנָּשְׂאוּ פִּתְחֵי עוֹלָם וְיָבוֹא מֶלֶךְ הַכָּבוֹד: מִי זֶה מֶלֶךְ הַכָּבוֹד אֲדֹנָי עִזּוּז וְגִבּוֹר אֲדֹנָי גִּבּוֹר מִלְחָמָה: שְׂאוּ שְׁעָרִים רָאשֵׁיכֶם וּשְׂאוּ פִּתְחֵי עוֹלָם וְיָבֹא מֶלֶךְ הַכָּבוֹד: מִי הוּא זֶה מֶלֶךְ הַכָּבוֹד אֲדֹנָי צְבָאוֹת הוּא מֶלֶךְ הַכָּבוֹד סֶלָה:

For David, a song. The earth and its fullness is God's, the world and those who dwell in it. For He founded it upon the seas and established it on the rivers. Who will go up on God's mountain and who will stand in His holy place? He that has clean hands and a pure heart, who has not taken My Name in vain nor sworn deceitfully. He shall receive a blessing from God and justice from the God of His salvation. This is the generation of those who seek Him, the offspring of Yaakov, who seek Your face. Selah. Lift up your heads, you gates, and be lifted up, you everlasting doors, and the King of Glory shall enter. Who is this King of Glory? God, strong and mighty, God, Who is mighty in battle. Lift up your heads, you gates, and lift them up, you everlasting doors, and the King of Glory will come in. Who is this King of Glory? God of Hosts, He is the King of Glory. Selah.

Psalm 42

לַמְנַצֵּחַ מַשְׂכִּיל לִבְנֵי קֹרַח: כְּאַיָּל תַּעֲרֹג עַל אֲפִיקֵי מָיִם כֵּן נַפְשִׁי תַעֲרֹג אֵלֶיךָ אֱלֹהִים: צָמְאָה נַפְשִׁי לֵאלֹהִים לְאֵל חָי מָתַי אָבוֹא וְאֵרָאֶה פְּנֵי אֱלֹהִים: הָיְתָה לִּי דִמְעָתִי לֶחֶם יוֹמָם וָלָיְלָה בֶּאֱמֹר אֵלַי כָּל הַיּוֹם אַיֵּה אֱלֹהֶיךָ: אֵלֶּה אֶזְכְּרָה וְאֶשְׁפְּכָה עָלַי נַפְשִׁי כִּי אֶעֱבֹר בַּסָּךְ אֶדַּדֵּם עַד בֵּית אֱלֹהִים בְּקוֹל רִנָּה וְתוֹדָה הָמוֹן חוֹגֵג: מַה תִּשְׁתּוֹחֲחִי נַפְשִׁי וַתֶּהֱמִי עָלָי הוֹחִלִי לֵאלֹהִים כִּי עוֹד אוֹדֶנּוּ

יְשׁוּעוֹת פָּנָיו: אֱלֹהַי עָלַי נַפְשִׁי תִשְׁתּוֹחָח עַל כֵּן אֶזְכָּרְךָ מֵאֶרֶץ יַרְדֵּן וְחֶרְמוֹנִים מֵהַר מִצְעָר: תְּהוֹם אֶל תְּהוֹם קוֹרֵא לְקוֹל צִנּוֹרֶיךָ כָּל מִשְׁבָּרֶיךָ וְגַלֶּיךָ עָלַי עָבָרוּ: יוֹמָם יְצַוֶּה אֲדֹנָי חַסְדּוֹ וּבַלַּיְלָה שִׁירֹה עִמִּי תְּפִלָּה לְאֵל חַיָּי: אוֹמְרָה לְאֵל סַלְעִי לָמָה שְׁכַחְתָּנִי לָמָּה קֹדֵר אֵלֵךְ בְּלַחַץ אוֹיֵב: בְּרֶצַח בְּעַצְמוֹתַי חֵרְפוּנִי צוֹרְרָי בְּאָמְרָם אֵלַי כָּל הַיּוֹם אַיֵּה אֱלֹהֶיךָ: מַה תִּשְׁתּוֹחֲחִי נַפְשִׁי וּמַה תֶּהֱמִי עָלָי הוֹחִילִי לֵאלֹהִים כִּי עוֹד אוֹדֶנּוּ יְשׁוּעֹת פָּנַי וֵאלֹהָי:

For the leader of the singers, a song to teach wisdom, for the sons of Korach. As the hart pants after streams of water, so my soul cries out for You, O God. My soul thirst for God, the living God: when will I come and appear in the presence of God? My tears have been my bread day and night, as my enemies taunt me all day long, asking, "Where is your God?" This I remember - and I pour out my soul within me - how I would go to Yerushalayim with the throngs for the festivals, how I would walk in the procession to the House of God with shouts of joy and thanks to God amidst the festival crowds. Why are you downcast, my soul? Why do you groan within me? Have hope in God. There will come a time when I will give thanks for the salvation which will come from His radiant presence. My God: My soul is downcast in this exile, as I remember Your miracles in the land of the Yarden [when the River Jordan became dry land], at the peaks of Mount Hermon [where you passed over our wrongdoing], and at the lowly mountain [Sinai, where you forgave us the sin of the golden calf. Yet in our present exile,] Deep cries out to deep, one sorrow cries out after another, with the cry from the channels through which You send punishments, which are poured out like water. All Your breakers and waves have swept over me. With the light of day let God command His kindness to be revealed. Even in the night of exile, may His presence rest with me. This is my prayer to the God of my life. I say to God, my Rock: Why have You forgotten me? Why must I go about in dark gloom under the oppression of the enemy? I feel it like murder in my bones when my oppressors taunt me and say to me all day, "Where is your God?" Why are you downcast, O my soul? Why do you groan within me? Have hope in God, for I will yet have cause to acknowledge Him, my salvation, the light of my face and my God.

Psalm 43

שָׁפְטֵנִי אֱלֹהִים וְרִיבָה רִיבִי מִגּוֹי לֹא חָסִיד מֵאִישׁ מִרְמָה וְעַוְלָה תְפַלְּטֵנִי: כִּי אַתָּה אֱלֹהֵי מָעוּזִּי לָמָה זְנַחְתָּנִי לָמָּה קֹדֵר אֶתְהַלֵּךְ בְּלַחַץ אוֹיֵב: שְׁלַח אוֹרְךָ וַאֲמִתְּךָ, הֵמָּה יַנְחוּנִי יְבִיאוּנִי אֶל הַר קָדְשְׁךָ וְאֶל מִשְׁכְּנוֹתֶיךָ: וְאָבוֹאָה אֶל מִזְבַּח אֱלֹהִים, אֶל אֵל שִׂמְחַת גִּילִי, וְאוֹדְךָ בְכִנּוֹר אֱלֹהִים אֱלֹהָי: מַה תִּשְׁתּוֹחֲחִי נַפְשִׁי, וּמַה תֶּהֱמִי עָלָי, הוֹחִילִי לֵאלֹהִים, כִּי עוֹד אוֹדֶנּוּ יְשׁוּעֹת, פָּנַי וֵאלֹהָי:

Judge me, O God, and plead my cause against an ungodly nation. Deliver me from deceitful and unjust men. For You are the God of my strength: Why do You abandon me? Why do I go about mourning under the oppression of the enemy? Send out Your Light and Your Truth: They will lead me; they will bring me to Your Holy Mountain and Your holy dwelling places. Then I will come to God's altar, to God, my happiness and joy, and I will give thanks to You with the lyre, O God, my God. Why are you downcast, my soul, and why do you moan within me? Hope in God! For I will yet thank Him for His salvations - He is the light of my face, and my God.

Psalm 20

לַמְנַצֵּחַ מִזְמוֹר לְדָוִד: יַעַנְךָ אֲדֹנָי בְּיוֹם צָרָה יְשַׂגֶּבְךָ שֵׁם אֱלֹהֵי יַעֲקֹב: יִשְׁלַח עֶזְרְךָ מִקֹּדֶשׁ וּמִצִּיּוֹן יִסְעָדֶךָּ: יִזְכֹּר כָּל מִנְחֹתֶךָ וְעוֹלָתְךָ יְדַשְּׁנֶה סֶלָה: יִתֶּן לְךָ כִלְבָבֶךָ וְכָל עֲצָתְךָ יְמַלֵּא: נְרַנְּנָה בִּישׁוּעָתֶךָ וּבְשֵׁם אֱלֹהֵינוּ נִדְגֹּל יְמַלֵּא אֲדֹנָי כָּל מִשְׁאֲלוֹתֶיךָ: עַתָּה יָדַעְתִּי כִּי הוֹשִׁיעַ אֲדֹנָי מְשִׁיחוֹ יַעֲנֵהוּ מִשְּׁמֵי קָדְשׁוֹ בִּגְבֻרוֹת יֵשַׁע יְמִינוֹ: אֵלֶּה בָרֶכֶב וְאֵלֶּה בַסּוּסִים וַאֲנַחְנוּ בְּשֵׁם אֲדֹנָי אֱלֹהֵינוּ נַזְכִּיר: הֵמָּה כָּרְעוּ וְנָפָלוּ וַאֲנַחְנוּ קַּמְנוּ וַנִּתְעוֹדָד: אֲדֹנָי הוֹשִׁיעָה הַמֶּלֶךְ יַעֲנֵנוּ בְיוֹם קָרְאֵנוּ:

For the leader of the singers. A song of David. God will answer you on the day of trouble; the Name of the God of Yaakov will strengthen you. He will send you help from the Sanctuary, and from Zion he will support you. He will remember all your offerings, and accept your burnt offering with favor. Selah. He will grant you your heart's desire, and fulfill all your counsel. We will rejoice in Your salvation, and make the Name of our God our banner. God will fulfill all your requests. Now I know that God saves His anointed, and will answer him from His Holy Dwellings in the Heavens with the saving strength of His arm. Some trust in chariots, and some in horses: but we will call on the Name of HaShem, our God. They have bent over and fallen, but we have risen and gained sway. God save us! The King will answer us on the day we call.

Psalm 67

לַמְנַצֵּחַ בִּנְגִינֹת מִזְמוֹר שִׁיר: אֱלֹהִים יְחָנֵּנוּ וִיבָרְכֵנוּ יָאֵר פָּנָיו אִתָּנוּ סֶלָה: לָדַעַת בָּאָרֶץ דַּרְכֶּךָ בְּכָל גּוֹיִם יְשׁוּעָתֶךָ: יוֹדוּךָ עַמִּים אֱלֹהִים יוֹדוּךָ עַמִּים כֻּלָּם: יִשְׂמְחוּ וִירַנְּנוּ לְאֻמִּים כִּי תִשְׁפֹּט עַמִּים מִישֹׁר וּלְאֻמִּים בָּאָרֶץ תַּנְחֵם סֶלָה: יוֹדוּךָ עַמִּים אֱלֹהִים יוֹדוּךָ עַמִּים כֻּלָּם: אֶרֶץ נָתְנָה יְבוּלָהּ יְבָרְכֵנוּ אֱלֹהִים אֱלֹהֵינוּ: יְבָרְכֵנוּ אֱלֹהִים וְיִירְאוּ אוֹתוֹ כָּל אַפְסֵי אָרֶץ:

For the leader of the singers. A Psalm, a Song. May God favor us and bless us, may He shine His countenance upon us, Selah! To make Your way known on earth and Your salvation among all the nations. Let the nations acknowledge You, O God: Let all the nations give thanks to You. The nations will be glad and sing for joy: For You will judge the nations fairly, and guide the nations on earth, Selah! Let the nations acknowledge You; O God, let all the nations give You thanks. The earth has yielded her produce. May God - our God bless us! And let all the ends of the earth fear Him.

Psalm 111

הַלְלוּיָהּ אוֹדֶה אֲדֹנָי בְּכָל לֵבָב בְּסוֹד יְשָׁרִים וְעֵדָה: גְּדֹלִים מַעֲשֵׂי אֲדֹנָי דְּרוּשִׁים לְכָל חֶפְצֵיהֶם: הוֹד וְהָדָר פָּעֳלוֹ וְצִדְקָתוֹ עֹמֶדֶת לָעַד: זֵכֶר עָשָׂה לְנִפְלְאֹתָיו חַנּוּן וְרַחוּם אֲדֹנָי: טֶרֶף נָתַן לִירֵאָיו יִזְכֹּר לְעוֹלָם בְּרִיתוֹ: כֹּחַ מַעֲשָׂיו הִגִּיד לְעַמּוֹ לָתֵת לָהֶם נַחֲלַת גּוֹיִם: מַעֲשֵׂי יָדָיו אֱמֶת וּמִשְׁפָּט נֶאֱמָנִים כָּל פִּקּוּדָיו: סְמוּכִים לָעַד לְעוֹלָם עֲשׂוּיִם בֶּאֱמֶת וְיָשָׁר: פְּדוּת שָׁלַח לְעַמּוֹ צִוָּה לְעוֹלָם בְּרִיתוֹ קָדוֹשׁ וְנוֹרָא שְׁמוֹ: רֵאשִׁית חָכְמָה יִרְאַת אֲדֹנָי שֵׂכֶל טוֹב לְכָל עֹשֵׂיהֶם תְּהִלָּתוֹ עֹמֶדֶת לָעַד:

HallelOyah! I will thank God wholeheartedly in the assembly of the upright, and in the congregation, the works of God are great, sought out by all who love them. Majesty and splendor are His work, and His righteousness endures forever. He has established reminders of His miracles: God is gracious and compassionate. He has given food to those who fear Him; He will always remember His covenant. He has declared to His people the power of His works, so that He may give them the heritage of the nations. The works of His hands are truth and justice; all His commandments are sure. They stand firm forever and ever, accomplished in truth and uprightness. He sent redemption to His people; He has commanded His covenant for ever; His Name is holy and awesome. The beginning of wisdom is fear of God; all who practice His Commandments have good understanding. His praise endures forever.

נוֹעַ תָּנוּעַ אֶרֶץ כַּשִּׁכּוֹר וְהִתְנוֹדְדָה כַּמְּלוּנָה וְכָבַד עָלֶיהָ פִּשְׁעָהּ וְנָפְלָה וְלֹא תֹסִיף קוּם: וְהָיָה בַּיּוֹם הַהוּא יִפְקֹד אֲדֹנָי עַל צְבָא הַמָּרוֹם בַּמָּרוֹם וְעַל מַלְכֵי הָאֲדָמָה עַל הָאֲדָמָה:

The earth will reel and totter as a drunkard. It will shake like a rickety hut. Its sins will weigh heavily upon it. It will fall and rise no more. And it shall be on that day God will settle the account with all the heavenly hosts on high and with all the leaders of the earth on earth (Isaiah 24:20-21).

Psalm 51

לַמְנַצֵּחַ מִזְמוֹר לְדָוִד: בְּבוֹא אֵלָיו נָתָן הַנָּבִיא כַּאֲשֶׁר בָּא אֶל בַּת שֶׁבַע: חָנֵּנִי אֱלֹהִים כְּחַסְדֶּךָ כְּרֹב רַחֲמֶיךָ מְחֵה פְשָׁעָי: הֶרֶב כַּבְּסֵנִי מֵעֲוֹנִי וּמֵחַטָּאתִי טַהֲרֵנִי: כִּי פְשָׁעַי אֲנִי אֵדָע וְחַטָּאתִי נֶגְדִּי תָמִיד: לְךָ לְבַדְּךָ חָטָאתִי וְהָרַע בְּעֵינֶיךָ עָשִׂיתִי לְמַעַן תִּצְדַּק בְּדָבְרֶךָ תִּזְכֶּה בְשָׁפְטֶךָ: הֵן בְּעָווֹן חוֹלָלְתִּי וּבְחֵטְא יֶחֱמַתְנִי אִמִּי: הֵן אֱמֶת חָפַצְתָּ בַטֻּחוֹת וּבְסָתֻם חָכְמָה תוֹדִיעֵנִי: תְּחַטְּאֵנִי בְאֵזוֹב וְאֶטְהָר תְּכַבְּסֵנִי וּמִשֶּׁלֶג אַלְבִּין: תַּשְׁמִיעֵנִי שָׂשׂוֹן וְשִׂמְחָה תָּגֵלְנָה עֲצָמוֹת דִּכִּיתָ: הַסְתֵּר פָּנֶיךָ מֵחֲטָאָי וְכָל עֲוֹנֹתַי מְחֵה: לֵב טָהוֹר בְּרָא לִי אֱלֹהִים וְרוּחַ נָכוֹן חַדֵּשׁ בְּקִרְבִּי: אַל תַּשְׁלִיכֵנִי מִלְּפָנֶיךָ וְרוּחַ קָדְשְׁךָ אַל תִּקַּח מִמֶּנִּי: הָשִׁיבָה לִי שְׂשׂוֹן יִשְׁעֶךָ וְרוּחַ נְדִיבָה תִסְמְכֵנִי: אֲלַמְּדָה פֹשְׁעִים דְּרָכֶיךָ וְחַטָּאִים אֵלֶיךָ יָשׁוּבוּ: הַצִּילֵנִי מִדָּמִים אֱלֹהִים אֱלֹהֵי תְּשׁוּעָתִי תְּרַנֵּן לְשׁוֹנִי צִדְקָתֶךָ: אֲדֹנָי שְׂפָתַי תִּפְתָּח וּפִי יַגִּיד תְּהִלָּתֶךָ: כִּי לֹא תַחְפֹּץ זֶבַח וְאֶתֵּנָה עוֹלָה לֹא תִרְצֶה: זִבְחֵי אֱלֹהִים רוּחַ נִשְׁבָּרָה לֵב נִשְׁבָּר וְנִדְכֶּה אֱלֹהִים לֹא תִבְזֶה: הֵיטִיבָה בִרְצוֹנְךָ אֶת צִיּוֹן תִּבְנֶה חוֹמוֹת יְרוּשָׁלִָם: אָז תַּחְפֹּץ זִבְחֵי צֶדֶק עוֹלָה וְכָלִיל אָז יַעֲלוּ עַל מִזְבַּחֲךָ פָרִים:

For the leader of the singers. A song of David. When Natan the prophet came to him after he had. Gone to Bat-Sheva.

Be kind to me, God, in accordance with Your mercy; in accordance with Your abundant compassion, blot out my transgressions. Wash me thoroughly from my inquiry and cleanse me from my sin. For I acknowledge my transgressions, and my sin. For I acknowledge my transgressions, and my sin is always before me. Against You alone have I sinned, and I have done that which is evil in Your sight, so that You are justified in Your sentence and righteous in Your judgment. Indeed, I was formed in iniquity and in sin did my mother conceive me. Surely You desire truth in our innermost being: therefore teach me wisdom deep in my heart. Purge me with hyssop and I shall be clean; wash me and I shall be whiter than snow. Let me hear gladness and joy; let the bones that You crush rejoice. Hide Your face from my sins and erase my iniquities. Create in me a pure heart, O God, and renew a steadfast spirit within me. Don't cast me away from Your presence and don't take Your holy spirit from me. Give me back the joy of Your salvation and support me with a willing spirit. I will teach transgressors Your ways, and sinners will return to You. Save me from bloodshed, O God, God of my salvation and my tongue will sing out loud about Your righteousness. O God, open my lips, and my mouth will tell Your praise. For You do not wish for a sacrifice, or else I would give it: You do not want a burnt offering. The sacrifices of God are a broken spirit - O God, You do not despise a broken and a contrite heart. Show goodness and favor to Zion; build the walls of Yerushalayim. Then You will favor the sacrifices of righteousness and whole burnt offerings: then bullocks will go up on Your altar.

Psalm 126

שִׁיר הַמַּעֲלוֹת בְּשׁוּב אֲדֹנָי אֶת שִׁיבַת צִיּוֹן הָיִינוּ כְּחֹלְמִים: אָז יִמָּלֵא שְׂחוֹק פִּינוּ וּלְשׁוֹנֵנוּ רִנָּה אָז יֹאמְרוּ בַגּוֹיִם הִגְדִּיל אֲדֹנָי לַעֲשׂוֹת עִם אֵלֶּה: הִגְדִּיל אֲדֹנָי לַעֲשׂוֹת עִמָּנוּ הָיִינוּ שְׂמֵחִים: שׁוּבָה אֲדֹנָי אֶת שְׁבִיתֵנוּ כַּאֲפִיקִים בַּנֶּגֶב: הַזֹּרְעִים בְּדִמְעָה בְּרִנָּה יִקְצֹרוּ: הָלוֹךְ יֵלֵךְ וּבָכֹה נֹשֵׂא מֶשֶׁךְ הַזָּרַע בֹּא יָבֹא בְרִנָּה נֹשֵׂא אֲלֻמֹּתָיו:

A Song of Ascents: When God brought back the captives of Zion we were like dreamers. Then our mouth was filled with laughter and our tongue with singing: then they said among the nations, "God has done great things for them." God has done great things for us: we were joyous. Bring back; our exiles, God,

Tikkun Shechinah

like streams of water in a dry land. Those who sow in tears will reap in joy. The one who goes on his way weeping, carrying a burden of seed, will certainly come back joyous, carrying his sheaves.

עַד אָנָה בְּכִיָּה בְּצִיּוֹן וּמִסְפֵּד בִּירוּשָׁלָיִם:

Until when will there be weeping in Zion and mourning in Yerushalayim?

תָּקוּם תְּרַחֵם צִיּוֹן וְתִבְנֶה חוֹמוֹת יְרוּשָׁלָיִם: אַתָּה תָקוּם תְּרַחֵם צִיּוֹן כִּי עֵת לְחֶנְנָהּ כִּי בָא מוֹעֵד: כִּי רָצוּ עֲבָדֶיךָ אֶת אֲבָנֶיהָ וְאֶת עֲפָרָהּ יְחֹנֵנוּ: (תהילים פרק קב) בּוֹנֵה יְרוּשָׁלַיִם אֲדֹנָי נִדְחֵי יִשְׂרָאֵל יְכַנֵּס: (תהילים קמז)

Arise! Have mercy on Zion and build the walls of Yerushalayim. You will arise and have mercy on Zion, for it is time to have pity on her, for the moment has come. For Your servants desire her stones, her very dust is precious to them (Psalms 102:14-15). God is the builder of Yerushalayim. He will gather in the dispersed of Israel (ibid. 147:2).

Tikkun Leah is followed by R. Chaim HaKohens beautiful poem, "My Beloved has gone down to His garden," written in the form of a dialog between the Holy One and Israel.

דּוֹדִי יָרַד לְגַנּוֹ לִרְעוֹת בַּגַּנִּים
לְהִשְׁתַּעֲשֵׁעַ וְלִלְקֹט שׁוֹשַׁנִּים
קוֹל דּוֹדִי דוֹפֵק פִּתְחִי לִי תַמָּתִי
שַׁעֲרֵי צִיּוֹן אֲשֶׁר אָהַבְתִּי

My Beloved has gone down to His garden to feed,
To play, and to gather roses.
The voice of my Beloved knocks: "Open for Me,
My perfect one, the gates of Zion that I love!"

אֵלֶיךָ דוֹדִי נַפְשִׁי אֶשָּׂא
אֵיךְ אֵשֶׁת נְעוּרִים הִיא גְרוּשָׁה
מֵאָז הָיִיתִי עַל לִבְּךָ חֲרוּשָׁה
וְעַתָּה הַמַּלְכָּתְּ אֵשֶׁת זְנוּנִים

[Israel:] To You, my beloved, I lift up my soul.
How has the wife of Your youth been driven out?
From the earliest time I was inscribed upon Your heart,

And now You have crowned the wanton woman!

בִּתִּי אַל תִּפְחֲדִי כִּי עוֹד אֶזְכְּרֵךְ
וּמֵאֶרֶץ רְחוֹקָה אֲקַבֵּץ פְּזוּרֵךְ
עוֹד אֶבְנֵךְ וְנִבְנֵית בְּיָפְיֵךְ וַהֲדָרֵךְ
וְגַם אָמְנָה אַתְּ אֲחוֹתִי

[God:] My daughter, fear not, for I will yet remember you,
And from a far-off land I will gather your dispersed.
I will yet build you, and you will be established in your beauty and splendor.
You are, after all, My sister.

גָּדֵל כְּאֵבִי כָּל עֵת אֶזְכְּרָה
אֵיכָה שִׁפְחָה תִירַשׁ גְּבִירָה
וְהִיא עַתָּה מִתְנַכֵּרָה
בְּשִׂמְחַת עוֹלָם וְנִטְעֵי נַעֲמָנִים

[Israel:] How great is my pain every time I recall
How the maidservant has usurped her mistress's place,
And now the mistress is estranged,
Though previously she was ever-joyful as the sapling of pleasant trees.

דְּעִי כִּי אֲחִישֶׁנָּה עֵת רָצוֹן
וְתִשְׁאֲבִי מַיִם חַיִּים בְּשָׂשׂוֹן
אֶשְׁלַח גְּדִי עִזִּים מִן הַצֹּאן
אֶל אֶרֶץ גְּזֵרָה בְּיַד אִישׁ עִתִּי [= מזומן]

[God:] Know that I will hasten the arrival of the time of favor,
And you will draw living waters in joy.
I will send the kid goat from the herds,
According to My decree, in the hands of a specially prepared man (Mashiach).

הָהּ הָהּ אֲדוֹנִי כִּי בְזִיתַנִי
וּמִשָּׁמַיִם אֶרֶץ הִשְׁלַכְתַּנִי
בְּיוֹם קָרָה מַעֲדֶה בֶּגֶד יְעַטַּנִי
וַאֲשֶׁר בֵּיתִי הָיָה לְבוּשׁ שָׁנִים

[Israel:] Ah! God! How You have humiliated me!
You cast me down from Heaven to the land of Seir.

Tikkun Shechinah

On that fateful day, I was divested of my garments,
Though formerly my household was clothed in scarlet.

וָאַלְבִּישֵׁךְ רִקְמָה וָשֵׁשׁ אֲחַבְּשֵׁךְ
וּמִשְׁבְּצוֹת זָהָב עַל לְבוּשֵׁךְ
וַעֲטֶרֶת תִּפְאֶרֶת תִּהְיֶה בְרֹאשֵׁךְ
וְעַל כָּל כָּבוֹד יָפָה אַתְּ רַעְיָתִי

[God:] But I will dress you in embroidered robes. I will wrap you in linen
And put gold settings on your vestments.
And a crown of splendor will be upon your head.
And with all the glory, "How beautiful you are, My beloved."

נָר טִמֵּא הֵיכַל קָדְשִׁי
בְּנֵי צִיּוֹן הַיְקָרִים לְנִבְלֵי חַרְשִׂי
עֵרוּ עֵרוּ יְסוֹד מִקְדָּשִׁי
עָבְרוּ עַל נַפְשִׁי מַיִם הַזֵּדוֹנִים

[Israel:] A felon has desecrated my Holy Sanctuary.
The precious sons of Zion were treated like cheap pottery.
My Temple was razed to the very foundations.
The turbulent waters have passed over me.

חֵץ יְפַלַּח סְגוֹר לְבָבָם
תַּחַת הַנְּחֹשֶׁת אָבִיא זָהָב
בָּנַיִךְ מֵרָחוֹק יָבִיאוּ עַל גַּבָּם
עֲתָרַי בַּת פּוּצַי יוֹבִילוּן מִנְחָתִי

[God:] An arrow will split the lock of their hearts.
Instead of copper, I will bring their gold.
From afar they will bring your sons on their backs.
The communities of My worshippers, whom I scattered, will bring My offering.

טָהוֹר אַתָּה לֹא אֵל חָפֵץ רֶשַׁע
עַד אָן לֹא תָבִיא צַדִּיק וְנוֹשָׁע
תָּשׁוּב וְתַלְבִּישֵׁנִי בִּגְדֵי יֶשַׁע
מְעִיל צְדָקָה וְרֹב פְּנִינִים

[Israel:] Pure One! You are not a God who desires evil.

Until when will You refrain from being the Righteous One, the Redeemer?
Return and clothe me in the garments of redemption -
A robe of charity with a multitude of pearls.

יְדִידוּת נַפְשִׁי מַה תִּתְאוֹנְנִי
צִדְקֵךְ גַּם אַהֲבָתֵךְ לֹא נִפְלֵאת מֶנִּי
מִיּוֹם גָּלוֹתֵךְ נָדַדְתִּי אָנִי
כְּצִפּוֹר נוֹדֶדֶת עָזַבְתִּי אֶת בֵּיתִי

[God:] Companion of My soul, why do you complain?
Your righteousness and love are not concealed from Me!
Indeed, from the day of your exile, I too became a wanderer.
Like a wandering bird I left My home.

כְּלוּם יֵשׁ הֲנָאָה מִבְּשַׂר חֲמוֹרִים
כִּי תִשְׁכַּח אַהֲבַת אֵשֶׁת נְעוּרִים
לַחְצֹב לְךָ בּוֹרוֹת כֻּלָּם נִשְׁבָּרִים
וְאֵין בָּהֶם מַיִם אַךְ רֹאשׁ פְּתָנִים

[Israel:] How can anyone delight in donkey's meat?
How can You forget the love of Your first wife,
And instead dig wells for Yourself that all crack asunder?
They contain no water, only snake's venom.

לָכֵן הַצַּדִּיק אָבַד עֵקֶב נְפִילָתֵךְ
וִימִינִי הוּשַׁב אָחוֹר מֵרֹב אַהֲבָתֵךְ
לֹא נִכְנַסְתִּי בְּבֵיתִי מִיּוֹם גָּלוּתֵךְ
לְבַל אֶרְאֶה בְּרָעָתִי

[God:] Therefore the Righteous One is also in exile as a result of your fall.
My right hand is held back because of My great love for you.
I have not entered My House from the day you were exiled,
So as not to be confronted with My overwhelming anguish.

מַלְכִּי קַנֵּא לִכְבוֹד שְׁכִינָתֶךָ
בְּעָלוּנוּ אֲדוֹנִים זָרִים זוּלָתֶךָ
וּבִמְקוֹם מִקְדָּשְׁךָ וְנַחֲלָתֶךָ
שָׂמוּ הָאֲשֵׁרִים וְהַחַמָּנִים

[Israel:] My King! Defend the honor of Your *Shechinah*!

Tikkun Shechinah

Uncaring masters have raped me!
In the place of Your Sanctuary, Your inheritance,
They have set idols and pagan images.

נָקָם אֶלְבַּשׁ וְשַׁלְהֶבֶתְיָה
וְאֶשְׂרוֹף בֵּית עֲכּוּ"ם וּבֵית הַמִּצְרִיָּה
אַשְׁכִּיר חִצִּי מִדַּם חָלָל וְשִׁבְיָה
וּתְהִי זֹאת נֶחָמָתִי

[God:] I will clothe Myself in vengeance and the flame of God,
And I will burn the house of idolatry and the shrine of the
Egyptian goddess.
I will make My arrows drunk with the blood of the fallen and
captives.
This will be My consolation.

סִפָּיִךְ אֶבְנֶה וּשְׁעָרַיִךְ אָרִים
וִיסַדְתִּיךְ סָבִיב סָבִיב בַּסַּפִּירִים
וְשַׂמְתִּי כַּדְכֹד שִׁמְשׁוֹתַיִךְ מְאִירִים
וּבְנֵי הַיִּצְהָר עַל רֹאשׁ גֵּיא שְׁמָנִים

I will build your thresholds and raise your gates,
I will bedeck you roundabout with sapphires.
I will illumine your windows with the light of jewels.
And the sons of Yitzhar will return to the peak of the Mount of
Olives.

עוּרִי עוּרִי לִבְשִׁי בִגְדֵּךְ צִיּוֹן
כִּי בָנַיִךְ אֶגְאַל עַם עָנִי וְאֶבְיוֹן
עוּרִי דַבְּרִי שִׁיר בִּבְנָיַן אַפִּרְיוֹן
הַשְׁמִיעִינִי קוֹלֵךְ תַּחַת אֲהָבָתִי

Arise! Arise! Don your garments, O Zion!
For I will redeem your sons, the poor and the needy.
Awaken! Sing your song in the holy sanctuary!
Let Me hear your voice for the sake of My love for you!

פְּנֵי אֵל תָּשׁוּרִי מֵרֹאשׁ אֲמָנָה
וְעֵינָיִךְ תְּשׁוּרֵךְ מֵרֵאשִׁית הַשָּׁנָה
וְחָמֵשׁ הַיָּדוֹת תִּהְיֶה לָךְ לִמְנָה
כֵּן דּוֹדִי בָּרוּךְ בֵּין הַבָּנִים

You will behold the countenance of God in the merit of your fathers, who were the first to believe in Me.
The eye of providence will watch over you from the beginning of the year,
And the five divisions (*Kohanim*, Levites, Israelites, Kings, Prophets) will be presented to you as your portion.
Then my Beloved will be blessed on the lips of the sons.

צוּף דְּבַשׁ יָזוּב אִמְרָתֵךְ וְשִׂיחֵךְ
תִּשְׁכַּח יְמִינִי אִם אֶשְׁכָּחֵךְ
וּלְהַעֲלוֹת תָּמִיד עַל רָצוֹן מִזְבְּחֵךְ
עַל מִשְׁכָּבִי בַלֵּילוֹת בִּקַּשְׁתִּי

[Israel:] Your words of Torah and your prayers will flow like sweet honey.
Let my right hand forget its skills if I forget you.
That the continual offering should go up on your altar and find favor -
This I request as I lie on My bed at night.

קוֹלֵךְ שָׁמַעְתִּי מַחֲמַד עֵינִי
אֶשְׁאַל מִנְּשִׁיקוֹת פִּיהוּ יִשָּׁקֵנִי
וִימִין חָשְׁקוֹ תְּחַבְּקֵנִי
נָגִילָה בִּנְאוֹת דֶּשֶׁא וּמַעְיַן גַּנִּים

I heard Your voice, delight of my eye.
I ask that He should kiss me with the kisses of His mouth,
And that You should embrace me with the right Hand I long for.
We will rejoice in green meadows and the spring flowing through the gardens.

רֵעִי לְכָה נַשְׁכִּימָה לַכְּרָמִים
שָׁם אֶתֵּן אֶת דּוֹדִי לָךְ אַהֲבַת עוֹלָמִים
כְּאָח לִי אֶשָּׁקְךָ נֶגֶד כָּל הָעַמִּים
אֶנְהָגְךָ אֶל בֵּית אִמִּי וְאֶל חֶדֶר הוֹרָתִי

Dear one, let us arise early and go down to the vineyards,
There I will give You my affection and eternal love.
Like a brother I will kiss You before all the nations,
I will lead You to my mother's house and to the chamber where I was conceived.

Tikkun Shechinah

שִׂפְתוֹתַיִךְ כַּלָּה צוּף יְזוּבוּן
וְעֵינַיִךְ יוֹנִים לֵב יֵיטִיבוּן
שְׁנֵי שָׁדַיִךְ רָצוֹן יִשְׁאָבוּן
שֶׁפַע חַסְדֵי דָוִד הַנֶּאֱמָנִים

[God:] Your lips, My bride, flow with nectar.
Your eyes are like doves, gladdening the heart.
Your two breasts draw forth My goodwill.
I recall King David's many, everlasting kindnesses.

תַּבַּעְנָה שְׂפָתַי כִּי אֲזַמְּרָה לָךְ
יְדִידוּת נַפְשִׁי וְלִבִּי אַחֲרַיִךְ הָלָךְ
אַהֲבַת נְעוּרִים זָכַרְתִּי לָךְ
לָכֵן בּוֹאִי שִׁכְבִי עִמִּי אֲחוֹתִי

My lips will sing and express your praise!
Beloved of My soul, My heart followed you.
I bear in mind the love of your youth.
And so cleave to Me, My sister!

מֹר וַאֲהָלוֹת בְּגָדַיִךְ
נֵרְדְּ וְכַרְכֹּם שְׁמָנַיִךְ
צְרוֹר הַמֹּר בֵּין שָׁדַיִךְ
פְּאֵר וְכָבוֹד כָּל עֲדָתִי

Your garments are scented with myrrh and aloe.
Your oils are perfumed with spikenard and saffron.
A bundle of myrrh lies between your breasts,
The splendor and glory of My entire congregation.

תַּעַן לְשׁוֹנִי שִׁיר בְּסוֹד יְשָׁרִים
עֵת יִשְׂמַח יִשְׂרָאֵל עִם אֵשֶׁת נְעוּרִים
וְהֵיכָל תִּנָּסֵד בְּרֹאשׁ הֶהָרִים
בְּשַׁעֲרֵי צִיּוֹן נָעוּף כַּיּוֹנִים

[Israel:] My tongue will sing a song in the company of the upright
At the time when Israel will rejoice with his first wife
And the sanctuary will be established at the pinnacle of all mountains.
At the gates of Zion we will soar like doves.

חַלּוּ גְבוּרֵי כֹחַ אֲסִי וּלְאֻמִּי

יוֹמָם וָלַיְלָה לָאֵל אַל תִּתְּנוּ דֳמִי
יִבְנֶה צִיּוֹן וִיכַנֵּס נִדְחֵי עַמִּי
מֵאַרְבַּע כַּנְפוֹת אֶל בֵּית חֶמְדָּתִי

Pray, mighty warriors, my brothers and my people!
Day and night give no respite to God,
Praying that He should build Zion and bring in the dispersed of my nation
From the four corners of the earth to the house of my desire.

כְּבוֹד יְיָ בְּתוֹכָהּ לְמוֹפֵת וּלְאוֹת
הָאֵשׁ חוֹמָה אֲרֻכָּה סָבִיב לְהַרְאוֹת
נָא חִישׁ גּוֹאֲלֵנוּ אֲדוֹן הַנִּפְלָאוֹת
הוֹשִׁיעָה יְמִינְךָ בְּיֶרַח הָאֵיתָנִים

God's glory will dwell in Zion as a sign and a wonder,
Seen as a long wall of fire all around.
Please hasten, our Redeemer, Master of Wonders!
Save us with Your right arm in the month of it powerful ones!

אֱלֹהֵינוּ וֵאלֹהֵי אֲבוֹתֵינוּ מֶלֶךְ רַחֲמָן רַחֵם עָלֵינוּ טוֹב וּמֵטִיב הִדָּרֶשׁ לָנוּ. שׁוּבָה אֵלֵינוּ בַּהֲמוֹן רַחֲמֶיךָ בִּגְלַל אָבוֹת שֶׁעָשׂוּ רְצוֹנֶךָ. בְּנֵה בֵיתְךָ כְּבַתְּחִלָּה וְכוֹנֵן מִקְדָּשְׁךָ עַל מְכוֹנוֹ. וְהַרְאֵנוּ בְּבִנְיָנוֹ וְשַׂמְּחֵנוּ בְּתִקּוּנוֹ. וְהָשֵׁב כֹּהֲנִים לַעֲבוֹדָתָם וּלְוִיִּם לְדוּכָנָם לְשִׁירָם וּלְזִמְרָם וְהָשֵׁב יִשְׂרָאֵל לִנְוֵיהֶם. וְשָׁם נַעֲלֶה וְנֵרָאֶה וְנִשְׁתַּחֲוֶה לְפָנֶיךָ. יְהִי רָצוֹן מִלְּפָנֶיךָ ה' אֱלֹהֵינוּ וֵאלֹהֵי אֲבוֹתֵינוּ שֶׁתַּעֲלֵנוּ בְשִׂמְחָה לְאַרְצֵנוּ וְתִטָּעֵנוּ בִּגְבוּלֵנוּ. וְשָׁם נַעֲשֶׂה לְפָנֶיךָ אֶת קָרְבְּנוֹת חוֹבוֹתֵינוּ תְּמִידִים כְּסִדְרָם וּמוּסָפִים כְּהִלְכָתָם:

      Our God and God of our fathers, loving King, have mercy on us. Good and beneficent God let Yourself be sought out by us. Return to us in Your abundant compassion for the sake of the patriarchs who did Your will Build Your House as at first and establish Your Sanctuary on its foundation. Show us its rebuilding and gladden us in its perfection. Restore the *Kohanim* to their service, the Levites to their platform, to their song and music, and restore Israel to their dwellings. And there let us go up and appear and prostrate before You. May it be Your will, HaShem our God and God of our fathers, to bring us up joyously to our land and to establish us in our borders, and there we will offer You the sacrifices that are incumbent upon us, the continual offerings according to their order and the additional offerings according to their Laws.

Tikkun Shechinah

It is customary to conclude Tikkun Chatzot with the recitation of the first chapter of Tractate __Tamid__, which describes the procedure in the Temple from midnight until the morning.

Mishnah 1

שְׁלֹשָׁה מְקוֹמוֹת הַכֹּהֲנִים שׁוֹמְרִים בְּבֵית הַמִּקְדָּשׁ, בְּבֵית אַבְטִינָס, בְּבֵית הַנִּיצוֹץ, וּבְבֵית הַמּוֹקֵד. בֵּית אַבְטִינָס וּבֵית הַנִּיצוֹץ הָיוּ עֲלִיּוֹת וְהָרוֹבִים שׁוֹמְרִים שָׁם. בֵּית הַמּוֹקֵד כִּפָּה וּבַיִת גָּדוֹל הָיָה, מוּקָף רוֹבְדִין שֶׁל אֶבֶן, וְזִקְנֵי בֵית אָב הָיוּ יְשֵׁנִים שָׁם, וּמַפְתְּחוֹת הָעֲזָרָה בְּיָדָם, וּפִרְחֵי כְהֻנָּה אִישׁ, וא' או ב' מהם היו נעורין במשמרות לשמור לא הָיוּ יְשֵׁנִים בְּבִגְדֵי קֹדֶשׁ, אֶלָּא פוֹשְׁטִין וּמְקַפְּלִין וּמַנִּיחִים אוֹתָם תַּחַת רָאשֵׁיהֶם, וּמִתְכַּסִּים בִּכְסוּת עַצְמָן. אֵרַע קֶרִי לְאֶחָד מֵהֶן, יוֹצֵא וְהוֹלֵךְ לוֹ בַּמְּסִבָּה הַהוֹלֶכֶת תַּחַת הַבִּירָה, וְהַנֵּרוֹת דּוֹלְקִין מִכָּאן וּמִכָּאן, עַד שֶׁהוּא מַגִּיעַ לְבֵית הַטְּבִילָה, וּמְדוּרָה הָיְתָה שָׁם, וּבֵית הַכִּסֵּא שֶׁל כָּבוֹד, וְזֶה הָיָה כְבוֹדוֹ, מְצָאוֹ נָעוּל בְּיָדוּעַ שֶׁיֵּשׁ שָׁם אָדָם; פָּתוּחַ בְּיָדוּעַ שֶׁאֵין שָׁם אָדָם. יָרַד וְטָבַל, עָלָה וְנִסְתַּפֵּג, וְנִתְחַמֵּם כְּנֶגֶד הַמְּדוּרָה. בָּא וְיָשַׁב לוֹ אֵצֶל אֶחָיו הַכֹּהֲנִים, עַד שֶׁהָיוּ הַשְּׁעָרִים נִפְתָּחִים, יוֹצֵא וְהוֹלֵךְ לוֹ.

There were three places in the Temple where the *Kohanim* stood watch: In the chamber of Avtinas, the chamber of Nitzut, and the Furnace Chamber. The chambers of Avtinas and Nitzutz were upper stories built next to the Temple courtyard, and the archers stood guard there. The Furnace Chamber was domed. It was a large chamber which had banks of hewn stone slabs protruding from the walls, and the elders of the priestly division which was on duty that night slept there, with the keys to the Temple courtyard in their hands. The young guard of the *Kohanim* also slept there, each one on his own mattress on the ground. They did not sleep in their priestly robes: They would take them off, fold them up and place them under their heads, sleeping in their own clothes.

If one of them had had an emission, he would go out through the passageway that went under the Temple Mount - it had lighted candles on both sides - until he reached the *mikvah*. It had a fireplace, and there was also a "seat of honor" (a restroom). The rule was that if he found it locked, it meant that someone was in there; if it was open, he knew there was no-one there. He would go down and immerse, get out of the water and dry himself, and warm himself up by the fireplace. He would come and sit with his fellow priests until the Temple gates were opened, when he would leave and go off [since the emission rendered him impure and unfit to serve for the entire day until nightfall].

Mishnah 2

מִי שֶׁהוּא רוֹצֶה לִתְרֹם אֶת הַמִּזְבֵּחַ, מַשְׁכִּים וְטוֹבֵל עַד שֶׁלֹּא יָבוֹא הַמְמֻנֶּה, וְכִי בְּאֵיזוֹ שָׁעָה הַמְמֻנֶּה בָא? לֹא כָל הָעִתִּים שָׁווֹת, פְּעָמִים שֶׁהוּא בָא מִקְרִיאַת הַגֶּבֶר, אוֹ סָמוּךְ לוֹ מִלְּפָנָיו אוֹ מִלְּאַחֲרָיו. הַמְמֻנֶּה בָא וְדוֹפֵק עֲלֵיהֶם, וְהֵם פּוֹתְחִין לוֹ. אָמַר לָהֶם, מִי שֶׁטָּבַל יָבוֹא וְיָפִיס. הֵפִיסוּ, זָכָה מִי שֶׁזָּכָה:

       Whoever wanted the *mitzvah* of taking off the ash from the altar would get up early and immerse even before the arrival of the officer in charge of the lottery. What time did the officer arrive? It was not always at the same time. He would arrive shortly before or after the crowing of the rooster. The officer would come and knock on the gate and they would open it for him. He would say, "Whoever has immersed should come and take part in the lottery." [To see who would take the ash from the altar]. The lottery was held, and whoever won, won.

Mishnah 3

נָטַל אֶת הַמַּפְתֵּחַ וּפָתַח אֶת הַפִּשְׁפָּשׁ, וְנִכְנַס מִבֵּית הַמּוֹקֵד לָעֲזָרָה, וְנִכְנְסוּ הַכֹּהֲנִים אַחֲרָיו, וּשְׁתֵּי אֲבוּקוֹת שֶׁל אוֹר בְּיָדָם, וְנֶחְלְקוּ לִשְׁתֵּי כִתּוֹת, אֵלּוּ מְהַלְּכִין בָּאַכְסַדְרָה דֶּרֶךְ הַמִּזְרָח, וְאֵלּוּ מְהַלְּכִין בָּאַכְסַדְרָה דֶּרֶךְ הַמַּעֲרָב, הָיוּ בּוֹדְקִין וְהוֹלְכִין, עַד שֶׁהֵם מַגִּיעִין לִמְקוֹם עוֹשֵׂי חֲבִתִּין, הִגִּיעוּ אֵלּוּ וָאֵלּוּ אָמְרוּ: שָׁלוֹם? הַכֹּל שָׁלוֹם; הֶעֱמִידוּ אֶת עוֹשֵׂי חֲבִתִּין לַעֲשׂוֹת חֲבִתִּין

       [The officer] took the key and opened the small gate and entered the courtyard. The *Kohanim* followed him with two lit torches in their hands. They split into two groups. One group went along the portico running eastwards, the other along the portico running westwards. They checked [to see that all the utensils were in their places] until they both came to the Bakery [where the High Priest's daily *Minchah* offering was prepared]. When they met, they said, "Peace! All is peace!" They appointed bakers to make the *Minchah* offering.

Mishnah 4

מִי שֶׁזָּכָה לִתְרֹם אֶת הַמִּזְבֵּחַ, הוּא יִתְרֹם וְהֵם אוֹמְרִים לוֹ הֱוֵי זָהִיר שֶׁלֹּא תִגַּע בִּכְלִי, עַד שֶׁתְּקַדֵּשׁ יָדֶיךָ וְרַגְלֶיךָ מִן הַכִּיּוֹר, וַהֲרֵי הַמַּחְתָּה נְתוּנָה בְּמִקְצוֹעַ בֵּין הַכֶּבֶשׁ לַמִּזְבֵּחַ, בְּמַעֲרָבוֹ שֶׁל כֶּבֶשׁ. אֵין אָדָם נִכְנָס עִמּוֹ, וְלֹא נֵר בְּיָדוֹ, אֶלָּא מְהַלֵּךְ לְאוֹר הַמַּעֲרָכָה. לֹא הָיוּ רוֹאִין אוֹתוֹ וְלֹא שׁוֹמְעִין אֶת קוֹלוֹ עַד שֶׁהָיוּ שׁוֹמְעִין קוֹל הָעֵץ, שֶׁעָשָׂה בֶן קָטִין מוּכְנִי לַכִּיּוֹר, וְהֵן אוֹמְרִים הִגִּיעַ עֵת. קִדֵּשׁ יָדָיו וְרַגְלָיו מִן הַכִּיּוֹר, נָטַל מַחְתַּת הַכֶּסֶף, וְעָלָה לְרֹאשׁ הַמִּזְבֵּחַ, וּפִנָּה אֶת הַגֶּחָלִים הֵילָךְ וְהֵילָךְ, וְחָתָה מִן הַמְאֻכָּלוֹת הַפְּנִימִיּוֹת וְיָרַד, הִגִּיעַ לָרִצְפָּה, הָפַךְ פָּנָיו לַצָּפוֹן, הָלַךְ לְמִזְרָחוֹ שֶׁל כֶּבֶשׁ כְּעֶשֶׂר אַמּוֹת, צָבַר אֶת הַגֶּחָלִים עַל גַּבֵּי הָרִצְפָּה, רָחוֹק מִן הַכֶּבֶשׁ שְׁלֹשָׁה טְפָחִים, מְקוֹם שֶׁנּוֹתְנִין שָׁם מֻרְאַת הָעוֹף וְדִשּׁוּן מִזְבַּח הַפְּנִימִי וְהַמְּנוֹרָה

The priest who won the lottery to clear the ashes would now do so, and they would tell him, "Be careful not to touch the shovel until you wash your hands and feet from the laver." The shovel was placed on the west side of the altar ramp, next to the altar. Nobody went in with him. He did not have a torch in his hand: He would see his way with the light of the fire of the altar. They could not see him or hear what he was doing until they heard the sound of the wooden lever that Ben Katin the mechanic made for [raising and lowering] the laver. They would then say, "It's time!"

He washed his hands and feet from the laver, took the silver shovel, went up to the top of the altar, and moved the coals to the sides. He would take some of the coals from the middle of the fire, which was well-burned. He then made his way down. When he reached the floor, he turned north and went about ten cubits along the east side of the ramp. He piled up the coals on the floor, three handbreadths from the ramp. This was where the crops of bird offerings were placed, as were the ashes from the incense, altar and *Menorah*.

PRAYERS AT CHATZOS BY REB MOSHE

2000 YEARS ARE ENOUGH, THE KOTEL CRIES OUT!

It has been 2000 years since I was erect and standing in my glory. I no longer see the Kohanim standing in their beautiful long robes. The Leveim, oh how I miss their beautiful songs. The simple Israelites, oh how I miss the way they served our Creator.
How much longer will it be? When will you repent and release me from imprisonment?
Hashem, Your people have been sighing over me for so many years. We want You Hashem and You only. Let the Torah and all the 613 mitzvos, those which we can complete in this exile and those reserved for the times of Mashiach, let them be completed. All the necessary rectifications should happen immediately, and we should see the Mashiach, mamash now!

Written, Cheshvan 1997

OY SALVATION

Hashem, You are always there for me, listening to and accepting my prayers. Oy, Hashem, my heart... aw, my body and soul cry out and feel sick. Help all of us; don't continue to turn us away. We are suffering too much from this bitter exile. Oy, if only You would bring us the salvation we long for. There are just too many people I know who are ill.
Please Hashem, it is enough suffering. Turn our mourning into gladness. Bring our limbs to burst out in dancing before You. Elevate our soul to a new madrega (level). Give us a complete salvation. We are Jews, Baruch Hashem. Hashem is One--the King, Helper, Deliverer, and our Shield. We shall lack nothing and tomorrow we will all be in Jerusalem, at the Bais Hamikdash (Temple). There we will dance and sing a new tune that will touch our hearts like never before. Hashem, we will be One and Your Name One.

Written, Adar bais, ches 1997

ARISE, CRY OUT!

Arise, cry out at night during the beginning of the watches! Pour out your heart like water in the presence of Hashem. Join the Malachim (angels) and the tzaddikim in praising HaKadosh BoruchHu during the most precious and beautiful watches. Just as the malachim of the past watch have stepped down from their posts, so must we push our previous thoughts and activities behind us. What a privilege it is to be awake at this precious hour. Please help me to use it to its fullest potential and not waste a precious moment of this beneficial time period. Assist me in truly learning Torah lishmah and praying to you with the utmost devotion. Others may sleep away their days (Psalms 59), ואני אשיר עזך *but as for me, I will sing of your strength* וארנן לבקר חסדך *and I will sing aloud in the morning of Your kindness.*

Written, 1997

AT NIGHT HIS SONG IS WITH ME

The kindness Hashem has given us by allowing us to open our mouths in prayer is beyond our comprehension. The only way to know your level of yiras Shamayim is by doing hisbodidus (meditation) in the mountain forest at chatzos (midnight). Your mouth will open, and words will flow forth to Hashem, similar to rains rushing down the mountainside. It is enough to go out to the forest for even a few minutes and yearn to be close to the Creator. For each time going, you will understand Chassidus greater and greater. The rebbes' (the Baal Shem Tov and Rebbe Nachman's) spirit will be real to you; their teachings will come alive like never before.

Chatzos is a time of great favor from Hashem and I shouldn't allow it to slip by. Help me, Hashem, to go to bed during the first watch of the night so I will be able to rise during the third one to praise You with the malachim (angels). I want to recite the Tikkun, do hisbodidus, learn Torah and make an evaluation of myself every night. May I never let this important time slip by without performing truthful avodas Hashem. My davening in the morning should not be affected by this devotion, nor the peace within my home.

יומם יצוה ה חסדו ובלילה שירה עימי תפילה לקל חי *During the day, Hashem's kindness is with me and during the night his song. May I look to Shamayim in the mornings and draw down daas (understanding). Thank You, Hashem, for giving us this special time in which we can serve You and draw near to You.*

Written, November 4, 1996

HOW MUCH LONGER?

Hashem, how much longer do we have to wait for the Bais HaMikdash (Temple) to be rebuilt? It has been so long that we are in exile, over 2000 years. We are lonely; mamash we are lonely and miss the holiness of the Bais HaMikdash. One stone of the Bais HaMikdash is more precious than all the jewels of the world.

Oh, to hear the Leveim singing and playing new songs to Hashem. Oh, to see the Kohanim dressed in the bigdei kahunah and the Yisraelim who are so dear to Hashem. To return home in peace and tranquility is my greatest dream. There could be just one curtain remaining in the kodssh hakadoshim waiting to be rectified [and then everything would be ready for the redemption.] (Baal Divrei Chaim).

Hashem, help us to do the remaining rectifications quickly and please, if we are just shy a little from its completion Hashem, You complete the rest for us. You have always helped us in our past trials; Hashem, we need You!

Nissan aleph 1997

Tikkun Shechinah

REBUILD OUR HOUSE!

Master of the World, Hashem, a house without the voices of children is destroyed more than the holy Temple. A house without joy and singing is empty. Too many people are suffering with barrenness and are alone.
How much longer must we continue to be tested until we have proven ourselves worthy of redemption? How long must we wait and cry bitter tears? Is our yearning not enough? How can we make ourselves a complete vessel for your holiness? Hashem, please lead us in the path of up-righteousness, purity and holiness. Hashem, when will we all gather together? Tzion is barren and desolate of the holiness it once had. We as a nation have suffered so greatly. We have been misjudged and emotionally scarred by the multitudes.
How can we elevate the remaining sparks? Unify that which is left and stuck in the unholy realms? When will we ourselves be unified? Bear fruit and break the shell? A town without the voices of children will be destroyed. Will the gates and doors we have now open to Yerushalayim? Has it rained on the garden enough? If not we, hasn't Hashem been lonely enough without His home glorified? Are all the righteous in Gan-Eden and this world not enough?
It is time! Mashiach is close! Let us yearn more than ever. Together with the righteous in Gan-Eden we can do it. We will soon be singing a new song! Each of our 248 limbs will dance before You, Hashem. We will soon be answered. Let us join together to bring the holy Mashiach. All of us as one, a nation of holiness. It will be just as the Rebono shel-Olom has promised.

Adar 7, 1997

GLOSSARY

ADNA - *ADNA* represents the *adon h'kol*-the Master of all. Name of Hashem, א-ד-נ-י
ADO-NOI
ARIZAL -Rabbi Isaac Luria
ASIYAH - The world of Action
ATZILUS - The world of Emmanation
AVODAS HASHEM - Service to G-D
AVOS- Patriarchs
BAIS HAMIKDOSH – The Holy Temple
BAIS MEDRASH - Jewish study hall located in a synagogue, yeshiva, kollel or other building
BARUCH HASHEM – Bless G-D
BESIM - Houses
BEN (BAS TORAH) - Someone who accepts to perform the Commandments in the Torah
BERIYAH - The world of Creation
BIKUR CHOLIM - Visiting the sick
BINAH – Understanding, One of the Ten Sefirot
BITUL - Nullified or selfless
BNAI YISRAEL - The children of Israel (Yaakov) also refers to the Jewish nation
BERACHOS - Blessings
CHAS V SHALOM - It shouldn't happen
CHASAN - Groom
CHEDER - Religious school for boys
CHEIN - Favor
CHOCHMAH - Wisdom
CHUPAH - Wedding Canopy the couple stands under during the ceremony
CHURBAN - Destruction
DAYAN - Judge
DERECH - Path
DEVEKUS - Referring to closeness to G-D
DOVID HAMELECH - King David
EMES - Truth
EMUNAH - Faith
ERETZ YISRAEL - Land of Israel
GADOLIM - Highly respected, very learned religious leaders; Torah Sages
GALUS - Diaspora, exile
GAN EDEN - Garden of Eden
GEHENAH - Underworld
GEMATRIA - Numerical value for letters and words
GEULAH - Redemption
GEVURAH – Severity, One of the Ten Sefirot
HALACHA - Jewish Law
HACHNASAS ORCHIM - Providing for or welcoming guests
HATZLACHA - Success
KEDUSHA - Holiness
KETER – Crown, One of the Ten Sefirot

189

KIRUV - Outreach
KLAL YISRAEL - The Jewish people
KLIPOS - Bad spirits
KOHANIM - Priestly class
MALACHIM - Angels
MALCHUS – Kingship, One of the Ten Sefirot
MAZALOS - Fortunes (zodiac signs)
MIDDA – Character trait
MIKVAH - Ritual bath house
MOHEL - Specialist who performs circumcisions
NACHAS - Joy
NEKUDOS - Vowels
NESHAMAH - Soul
NETZACH, HOD AND YESOD - Eternity, glory and foundation. Part of the Ten Sefiros
PARNASA - Income or livelihood
POSUKIM - Verses
POSUL -Unusable
SEFIROS - Emanations
SHEKIYA - Nightfall
SHEMONEH ESREH - 18 prayers said three times daily as part of the service
SHEVA BRACHOS - Seven feasts held for seven nights after the wedding, where the couple is blessed by attendees
SHIURIM - Speeches
SHOCHET - Butcher
TEFILLIN - Holy Scriptures wrapped in a box with leather straps to attach to the head and arm
TEFILLOS - Prayers
TEHILLIM - Psalms
TIFERES - Beauty, One of the Ten Sefirot
TIKKUN OLOM - Repair the world
TIKKUN (TIKKUNIM) - Repairing
TIKKUNEI ZOHAR - Main book of *Kabbalah* written by Rabbi Shimon Bar Yochai
TZADDIKIM - Righteous Persons
TZITZIS - Four cornered garment with strings attached to each corner
YICHUDIM - Unifications
YESHIVOS - Where boys learn Torah from high school and onwards
YETZER HARA - Evil inclination
YETZIRAH -The world of Formation
YIRAS HASHEM -Fear of God

Made in the USA
Lexington, KY
16 October 2018